ACTIVATING NIGERIA'S PROPHETIC CALL

A 21-DAY PRAYER GUIDE

On Cover: The Black Crowned Crane (Balearica pavonina) - is the Official "National bird of Nigeria". It's a symbol of elegance and dignity.[1]

J P J B E N T

Printed in Nigeria

ISBN-13: 978-0-620-81933-6

Published by:

MALUBA PUBLISHING

All scripture quotations are taken from the
Holy Bible, King James Version and
The New Living Translation
unless otherwise stated.

Cover Concept by JPJ Bent
Cover Design by Dhemian Art

Printed by
Printhiveng, a brand of
Heranchy Company

DEDICATION

To late Mrs. Mary Kande Bent (nee Tarfa), my praying mum who relentlessly prayed me into the Kingdom and became my very first prayer drill sergeant.

To all who still believe in Nigeria

ISBN-13: 978-0-620-81933-6

ACKNOWLEDGMENT

To my wife and my darling for 21 years
and going strong, my 'Dilly Dora' -
Olajumoke Dora Bent (nee Oluwasola)
and my most amazing prayer partner
Thank you for believing in me.

To all my prayer partners and prayer
groups over the years who have
contributed to shaping and sharpening
me into the praying man I am today.

CONTENT

CONTENT

INTRODUCTION

THE SPIRIT OF PROPHECY

It's important to understand the spirit of prophecy as it relates to the prominence of prophecy in the Bible.

The Bible is a prophetic and living book as no other book found on earth. This is because of the unique way the scriptures were written; with God as the author and men as the writers.

2 Timothy 3:16

"All scripture is given by inspiration of God, and is profitable for doctrine, for reproof, for correction, for instruction in righteousness"

2 Peter 1:19-21

"We have also a more sure word of prophecy; whereunto ye do well that ye take heed, as unto a light that shineth in a dark place, until the day dawn, and the day star arise in your hearts: Knowing this first that no prophecy of the scripture is of any private interpretation. For the prophecy came not in old time by the will of man: but holy men of God spake as they were moved by the Holy Ghost."

Two Categories of Prophecy

There are two basic categories:

Unconditional prophecies. Nothing can change them as God has predetermined that they must happen.

Conditional prophecies. These can change if the critical conditions are not met. All personal prophecies are conditional prophecies and certain conditions must be met by man for these to come to pass. These include personal prophecies to a people, a family and to an individual. Absolute obedience and right timing are usually the major keys in this case.

A prophetic word can have both categories of prophecies in it. The recipients are responsible to note the difference so they can respond correctly.

Example of Unconditional and Conditional Prophecies

The bondage and deliverance of the Israelites in Egypt provides a good example.

Genesis 18:13-14

"And he said unto Abram, Know of a surety that thy seed shall be a stranger in a land that is not theirs, and shall serve them; and they shall afflict them four hundred years;

And also that nation, whom they shall serve, will I judge: and afterward shall they come out with great substance."

Unconditional elements of the prophecy. The four hundred years of slavery in Egypt was unconditional. The judgment of the nation that would afflict them was non-negotiable and their coming out with great wealth was also unconditional.

Conditional elements of the prophecy. The individual players that would bring about the actual deliverance could change. So if Moses had refused to obey God, then God would have had to use someone else. Unfortunately so many didn't fulfil their personal prophecies of getting into the Promised Land due to unbelief; Joshua and Caleb were the only ones from their generation to make it out of Egypt and into the Promised Land.

An example of those who failed to fulfil their personal prophecies:
Eli the High Priest

1 Samuel 2:30
"Therefore the Lord God of Israel says: 'I said indeed that your house and the house of your father would walk before Me forever.' But now the Lord says: 'Far be it from Me; for those who honor Me I will honor, and those who despise Me shall be lightly esteemed.

An example of those who fulfilled their personal prophecies:
Joseph

Genesis 42:6, 9
"Now Joseph was governor over the land; and it was he who sold to all the people of the land. And Joseph's brothers came and bowed down before him with their faces to the earth. Then Joseph remembered the dreams which he had dreamed about them, and said to them, “You are spies! You have come to see the nakedness of the land!”

THE OFFICE OF THE PROPHET
Amos 3:7
"Surely the Lord God will do nothing, but he revealeth his secret unto his servants the prophets."
This is the oldest and most common office found in the Bible. Abel is the first in the long list of those called to be prophets.

Luke 11:49-51

"Therefore also said the wisdom of God, I will send them prophets and apostles, and some of them they shall slay and persecute: That the blood of all the prophets, which was shed from the foundation of the world, may be required of this generation; From the blood of Abel unto the blood of Zacharias, which perished between the altar and the temple: verily I say unto you, It shall be required of this generation."

The offices of prophets, kings and priests are common in both Old and New Testaments. However in the New Testament only the office of the prophet forms part of the five principal officers of the Church, which are: apostle, prophet, evangelist, pastor and teacher. While, the offices of kings and priests are roles all saints now share as joint-heirs with the Lord Jesus Christ and will continue to share through all eternity.

Revelation 5:10

"And hast made us unto our God kings and priests: and we shall reign on the earth."

The central role prophets and prophecies play in the Bible should tell us the critical importance of understanding prophecies. To be a good bible student, you must understand the place of prophets and prophecies.

The difference between the Gift of Prophecy and the Spirit of Prophecy

There is a difference between the gift of prophecy mentioned in 1Corinthians 12:10 and the spirit of prophecy mentioned in Revelation 19:10.

1 Corinthians 12:10

"To another the working of miracles; to another prophecy; to another discerning of spirits; to another divers kinds of tongues; to another the interpretation of tongues:"

Revelation 19:10

"And I fell at his feet to worship him. And he said unto me, See thou do it not: I am thy fellow servant, and of thy brethren that have the testimony of Jesus: worship God: for the testimony of Jesus is the spirit of prophecy."

The first basic difference is that the gift of prophecy operates through one person at a time, while the spirit of prophecy can operate upon multiple people at the same time and usually at a more powerful and more compelling dimension as compared to the gift of prophecy. The gift of prophecy requires the exercising of the personal faith of the speaker, while the spirit of prophecy though activated through the faith of one, usually does not require the faith or even the cooperation of all those required for its fulfilment.

Example of the Gift of Prophecy

Acts 21:10-11

"And as we tarried there many days, there came down from Judaea a certain prophet, named Agabus. And when he was come unto us, he took Paul's girdle, and bound his own hands and feet, and said, Thus saith the Holy Ghost, So shall the Jews at Jerusalem bind the man that owneth this girdle, and shall deliver him into the hands of the Gentiles."

Example of the Spirit of Prophecy

1 Samuel 19:18-24

"So David fled, and escaped, and came to Samuel to Ramah, and told him all that Saul had done to him. And he and Samuel went and dwelt in Naioth. And it was told Saul, saying, Behold, David is at Naioth in Ramah. And Saul sent messengers to take David: and when they saw the company of the prophets prophesying, and Samuel standing as appointed over them, the Spirit of God was upon the messengers of Saul, and they also prophesied. And when it was told Saul, he sent other messengers, and they prophesied likewise. And Saul sent messengers again the third time, and they prophesied also. Then went he also to Ramah, and came to a great well that is in Sechu: and he asked and said, Where are Samuel and David? And one said, Behold, they be at Naioth in Ramah. And he went thither to Naioth in Ramah: and the Spirit of God was upon him also, and he went on, and prophesied, until he came to Naioth in Ramah. And he stripped off his clothes also, and prophesied before Samuel in like manner, and lay down naked all that day and all that night. Wherefore they say, Is Saul also among the prophets?"

The Spirit of Prophecy in the life of Elisha

Elisha declares the word of prophecy loud and clear

2 Kings 7:1-2

"Then Elisha said, "Hear the word of the LORD. Thus says the Lord: 'Tomorrow about this time a seah of fine flour shall be sold for a shekel, and two seahs of barley for a shekel, at the gate of Samaria.'"

So an officer on whose hand the king leaned answered the man of God and said, "Look, if the LORD would make windows in heaven, could this thing be?" And he said, "In fact, you shall see it with your eyes, but you shall not eat of it."

The fulfilment of Elisha's prophecy
The spirit of prophecy moves upon the least likely men.

2 Kings 7:3-5
"Now there were four leprous men at the entrance of the gate; and they said to one another, "Why are we sitting here until we die? If we say, 'We will enter the city,' the famine is in the city, and we shall die there.And if we sit here, we die also. Now therefore, come, let us surrender to the army of the Syrians. If they keep us alive, we shall live; and if they kill us, we shall only die." And they rose at twilight to go to the camp of the Syrians; and when they had come to the outskirts of the Syrian camp, to their surprise no one was there."

The four lepers were sitting by the CITY GATE and were well out of hearing range of Prophet Elisha's prophecy. They were the ones that stepped out and unknown to them they were acting by the spirit of prophecy, while none of those who were standing physically by prophet Elisha acted on the Word. This means proximity is not always a guarantee for profitability. How did the four lepers act on a word they never heard audibly? This is because the prophetic declaration was conveyed by the spirit of prophecy to their spirits and they acted on it. The physical ear is not the same as the spiritual ear.

The spirit of prophecy moves against the camp of the Syrians

2 Kings 7:6-7

"For the Lord had caused the army of the Syrians to hear the noise of chariots and the noise of horses--the noise of a great army; so they said to one another, "Look, the king of Israel has hired against us the kings of the Hittites and the kings of the Egyptians to attack us!" Therefore they arose and fled at twilight, and left the camp intact--their tents, their horses, and their donkeys and they fled for their lives."

Amazingly the Syrian camp heard the sound of chariots at the twilight, which was the same time the four lepers rose to go into the camp. The spirit of prophecy came upon the camp and caused them to hear the sound of the chariots. It was so terrifying and so real that they fled on foot in such a panic that they didn't even use their horses and donkeys which would have been a much faster escape.

The spirit of prophecy then moved upon the Israelites who stormed the deserted enemy camp and the long famine was finally over in just 24 hours.

2 Kings 7:16

"Then the people went out and plundered the tents of the Syrians. So a seah of fine flour was sold for a shekel, and two seahs of barley for a shekel, according to the word of the Lord."

The spirit of prophecy moved upon the people and there was a stampede with an outcome in line with the word of the prophet.

2 Kings 7:17

"Now the king had appointed the officer on whose hand he leaned to have charge of the gate. But the people trampled him in the gate, and he died, just as the man of God had said, who spoke when the king came down to him." The people in a frenzied stampede ran over the right hand man of the king and he was the only one who died on the day of good news according to the words of Elisha.

Kindly notice that every aspect of the prophecy was fulfilled 100%.

The Spirit of Prophecy in the life of Cyrus
Prophet Isaiah Declares the prophecy

Isaiah 44:24-28
"Thus saith the Lord, thy redeemer, and he that formed thee from the womb, I am the Lord that maketh all things; that stretcheth forth the heavens alone; that spreadeth abroad the earth by myself; That frustrateth the tokens of the liars, and maketh diviners mad; that turneth wise men backward, and maketh their knowledge foolish; That confirmeth the word of his servant, and performeth the counsel of his messengers; that saith to Jerusalem, Thou shalt be inhabited; and to the cities of Judah, Ye shall be built, and I will raise up the decayed places thereof: That saith to the deep, Be dry, and I will dry up thy rivers: That saith of Cyrus, He is my shepherd, and shall perform all my pleasure: even saying to Jerusalem, Thou shalt be built; and to the temple, Thy foundation shall be laid."

Isaiah 45:1-3
"Thus saith the Lord to his anointed, to Cyrus, whose right hand I have holden, to subdue nations before him; and I will loose the loins of kings, to

open before him the two leaved gates; and the gates shall not be shut; I will go before thee, and make the crooked places straight: I will break in pieces the gates of brass, and cut in sunder the bars of iron: And I will give thee the treasures of darkness, and hidden riches of secret places, that thou mayest know that I, the Lord, which call thee by thy name, am the God of Israel."

These Prophecies by Prophet Isaiah about King Cyrus were declared about 150 years before Cyrus was born and about 200 years before their actual fulfilment.[2]

The fulfilment of Isaiah's prophecy

Ezra 1:1-4

"Now in the first year of Cyrus king of Persia, that the word of the Lord by the mouth of Jeremiah might be fulfilled, the Lord stirred up the spirit of Cyrus king of Persia, that he made a proclamation throughout all his kingdom, and put it also in writing, saying, Thus saith Cyrus king of Persia, The Lord God of heaven hath given me all the kingdoms of the earth; and he hath charged me to build him an house at Jerusalem, which is in Judah. Who is there among you of all his people? his God be with him, and let him go up to Jerusalem, which is in Judah, and build the house of the Lord God of Israel, (he is the God,) which is in Jerusalem. And whosoever remaineth in any place where he sojourneth, let the men of his place help him with silver, and with gold, and with goods, and with beasts, beside the freewill offering for the house of God that is in Jerusalem."

Cyrus was the son of Queen Esther, he was taught the word of God by his mother, his grand uncle Mordecai and prophet Nehemiah.[3] These prophecies were given so as to enable Cyrus fulfill Prophet Jeremiah's prophecy.

Jeremiah 25:9-12
"Behold, I will send and take all the families of the north, saith the Lord, and Nebuchadnezzar the king of Babylon, my servant, and will bring them against this land, and against the inhabitants thereof, and against all these nations round about, and will utterly destroy them, and make them an astonishment, and an hissing, and perpetual desolations. Moreover I will take from them the voice of mirth, and the voice of gladness, the voice of the bridegroom, and the voice of the bride, the sound of the millstones, and the light of the candle. And this whole land shall be a desolation, and an astonishment; and these nations shall serve the king of Babylon seventy years. And it shall come to pass, when seventy years are accomplished, that I will punish the king of Babylon, and that nation, saith the Lord, for their iniquity, and the land of the Chaldeans, and will make it perpetual desolations."

This is an awesome example of the power and interconnectivity of true prophecies that enables us know that there is no way such prophecies with some spanning over decades, centuries and even millennial can be manipulated by man. Their fulfilment had to be orchestrated by God Himself.

Prophet Daniel's role in the fulfilment of Jeremiah's prophecy

Daniel 9:1-3
"In the first year of Darius the son of Ahasuerus, of the lineage of the Medes, who was made king over the realm of the Chaldeans in the first year of his

reign I, Daniel, understood by the books the number of the years specified by the word of the Lord through Jeremiah the prophet, that He would *acc*omplish seventy years in the desolations of Jerusalem. Then I set my face toward the Lord God to make request by prayer and supplications, with fasting, sackcloth, and ashes."

Here we see God raising Prophet Daniel to act as a watchman and to prayerfully set the atmosphere for the fulfilment of Jeremiah's prophecy concerning the seventy years captivity of the Israelites in Babylon.
Without this keen intervention by Daniel, his people would have lingered in captivity a little longer than necessary.

This Daniel's prayer shows us a prophetic pattern that before God does any significant thing on the earth and in any nation He will first send the Spirit of Prophecy to prepare the people.

All true prophecies from God will be greatly opposed

Ezra 4:4-6
"Then the people of the land weakened the hands of the people of Judah, and troubled them in building, And hired counsellors against them, to frustrate their purpose, all the days of Cyrus king of Persia, even until the reign of Darius king of Persia. And in the reign of Ahasuerus, in the beginning of his reign, wrote they unto him an accusation against the inhabitants of Judah and Jerusalem."

Ezra 4:23-24
"Now when the copy of king Artaxerxes' letter was read before Rehum, and

Shimshai the scribe, and their companions, they went up in haste to Jerusalem unto the Jews, and made them to cease by force and power. Then ceased the work of the house of God which is at Jerusalem. So it ceased unto the second year of the reign of Darius king of Persia."
The role of other prophets in stirring the people to resume work and fulfill the prophecy

Ezra 5:1-2
"Then the prophets, Haggai the prophet, and Zechariah the son of Iddo, prophesied unto the Jews that were in Judah and Jerusalem in the name of the God of Israel, even unto them. Then rose up Zerubbabel the son of Shealtiel, and Jeshua the son of Jozadak, and began to build the house of God which is at Jerusalem: and with them were the prophets of God helping them."

Ezra 6:14-15
"And the elders of the Jews builded, and they prospered through the prophesying of Haggai the prophet and Zechariah the son of Iddo. And they builded, and finished it, according to the commandment of the God of Israel, and according to the commandment of Cyrus, and Darius, and Artaxerxes king of Persia. And this house was finished on the third day of the month Adar, which was in the sixth year of the reign of Darius the king."

These examples reveal the role of prophets throughout the lifespan of prophecies until their fulfilment. That's why God sent prophets Haggai and Zechariah to prophesy and stir up the people to action after the work was successfully halted by their enemies for about 18 years. If people don't respond to prophecies correctly, they could miss God's visitation although the prophecy will eventually come true but through another generation. It's absolutely important to note that there is no way any true prophecy over us as a nation or over you as an individual will come to pass without having to overcome a strong satanic opposition. It was true in Scripture and it's true today. That's why Paul told Timothy to use the prophecies to wage a good warfare **(1 Timothy 1:18).**

Generations that missed God's prophetic window

Joshua's generation missed their prophetic timing.
The Jews in the time of Jesus missed their prophetic window.

How the Spirit of Prophecy is activated

The Spirit of Prophecy is usually activated through the office of an established prophet and it influences whoever is needed to fulfil God's intent. God will do nothing on the earth, in your family, in your city, nation, continent, or generation without first seeking to reveal it to His prophetic point person.

Amos 3: 7-8

"Surely the Lord God does nothing, Unless He reveals His secret to His servants the prophets. A lion has roared! Who will not fear? The Lord God has spoken! Who can but prophesy?"

The above scripture reveals a definite divine pattern God employs in every generation. May we not be a deaf generation but may we hear the shout of the King amongst us loud and clear.

Numbers 23:21

"He has not observed iniquity in Jacob, nor has He seen wickedness in Israel. The Lord his God is with him, and the shout of a King is among them."

However if there are no spiritually keen people like Noah, Abraham, Joseph, or Daniel, then unfortunately the visitation of judgment will take the people by surprise.

All the books of the bible were written by the move of the spirit of prophecy of which the books written by the prophets particularly demonstrate this powerful pattern.

Outstanding manifestation can be seen in the books of Daniel, Isaiah, zekiel and the book of Revelations.

The Spirit of Prophecy always points to Jesus Christ, because it is upon Him that everything rises and falls.

Revelation 19:10

"And I fell at his feet to worship him. And he said unto me, See thou do it not: I am thy fellow servant, and of thy brethren that have the testimony of Jesus: worship God: for the testimony of Jesus is the spirit of prophecy."

ABOUT THE BLACK CROWNED CRANE

The Black Crowned Crane as featured on the cover of this book is Nigeria's National Bird. Amazingly not many Nigerians know this, just like so much is yet to be known of the greatness of this most populous African nation. This bird is elegant, colorful, flamboyant and stands out just like most Nigerians wherever they are found.

Sadly this bird is on the endangered species list and to the author this relates perfectly with the theme of this book which speaks of God prophetically calling Nigeria from the brink into her divine destiny.

HOW TO APPROACH THIS BOOK

As you proceed to the main section of this prayer guide, you need to be mindful of the background laid in this introduction.

Approach it prayerfully and with the right prophetic orientation so you can make the most of the truths contained there in. The author recommends that rather than just reading through the book, that the reader sets aside three weeks to read daily. Taking one chapter each day and then spending quality time in prayer and study of scripture. This cycle of three weeks can be repeated as often as desired.

My prayer for you is that you will be led by God's Spirit to fulfil your part in Heaven's prophetic intent to birth a new Nigeria.

God bless you and God bless Nigeria!

WEEK ONE

FIRST PROPHECY ON THE FIVE KINDS OF NIGERIANS (RECEIVED 2012)

BACKGROUND: SPIRITUAL MAPPING OF NIGERIANS

In 2012 the LORD gave me a prophetic description of the five kinds of Nigerians. This has nothing to do with the difference in ethnicity, language, religion or gender. It was a spiritual mapping of the spiritual groupings of Nigerians as of the time this prophecy was received.

Reference will be made throughout this devotional on the five kinds of Nigerians

PROPHECY: THE FIVE KINDS OF NIGERIANS

The Watchmen

Intercessors on the wall and it includes both men and women. These are a very critical group as they can see ahead of the rest and therefore warn of approaching calamity and avert many a disaster. But woe is the land if this group falls asleep or fails to sound the trumpet.

The Warriors

Reformers on the ground located in all the various fields of life. Most times the reformers are watchmen first but there are some watchmen that are not reformers.

This group are mostly made up of young and middle aged leaders and they are the ones engaged in the battle with the enemy and carry out the work of reformation and transformation (dividing the inheritance) like Joshua.

The Wasters

As their name implies, they are the ones wasting the land, wasting its resources and wasting the people in it. They waste and waste and waste with no intention, desire or plan to stop.

Their appetites increase with every succeeding generation of wasters. And, they form a very effective lineage of wasters. This is currently the strongest group and they must be stopped for they have a covenant with hell to waste the land and they are serious about it.

The challenge with this group is that they are a very infectious group and have rubbed off on all the other groups. Their craft once learnt is highly addictive and difficult to break off. This group is so effective that those they infect in the other groups don't have to change groups but will become wasters in that group. The three motivating characteristics of this group is excessive greed, extreme pride & exceptional self-importance. Isaiah 59 gives a bleak picture of what happens when the wasters are running the affairs of a nation.

The Worried Ones

The majority of the oppressed with no might or power to withstand the wasters. They are overwhelmed and have no clue on the way out or the way forward. They are the captives and the prey who are at the unfortunate 'mercy' of their merciless oppressors.

The Wise Ones

These are the Moses, Aaron and Hur on the mountain giving wisdom and direction to Joshua (warriors/reformers) on the way to victory. These ought to be the leaders in authority or counsellors surrounding the throne.

They are anointed by God and filled with divine wisdom to lead the nation into victory and into the Promised Land. Presently this is the most deficient of all the groups. The land has very few wise ones and their influence is dwindling and near extinction.

For every great throne or land must have its wise men around the throne but when that is lacking, then folly is enthroned, then anarchy and bondage knocks on the door. Bondage always comes with deprivation, groaning and pain. But for the few wise ones the land would have long been divided and disintegrated.

This group is what all the warriors ought to evolve into but sadly most warriors end up in the wrong group and become either Watchmen only or Worried Ones or even Wasters rather than become Sages to lead the next generation.

Be careful to discern this group accurately for there are two types of wise ones:

Wise men of Babylon. The wise ones of Babylon are planted by the enemy but are actually 'wasters' to bring about his agenda for the nation, people and generation. These ones are contrary to Christ's Kingdom and culture.

Wise men of the kingdom. The wise ones of the kingdom are planted by God like Daniel to influence the throne and bring about God's agenda for the nation, people and generation.

For every throne that is surrounded by wise ones, the nation will either prosper spiritually or be a spiritual reproach depending on which of these two is in charge.

1

THE FIVE KINDS OF NIGERIANS

CHAPTER ONE
PRAYER DAY 1

THE FIVE KINDS OF NIGERIANS

Prayer Quote

"Don't pray when you feel like it. Have an appointment with the Lord and keep it. A man is powerful on his knees."

Corrie ten Boom

Watchmen

Isaiah 62:6-7 NLT

"O Jerusalem, I have posted watchmen on your walls; they will pray day and night, continually. Take no rest, all you who pray to the Lord.
Give the Lord no rest until he completes his work, until he makes Jerusalem the pride of the earth."

Ezekiel 3:17 NLT

"Son of man, I have appointed you as a watchman for Israel. Whenever you receive a message from me, warn people immediately."

Prayer Point 1

- Pray that the Watchmen of Nigeria (you and I included) will rise to the occasion and not fail.
- Pray that the Lord Himself will direct and coordinate all the prayer efforts of the various watchmen He has placed upon the walls of Nigeria to STAND upon our watches until we experience His deliverance.

Jeremiah 31:6 NLT

"The day will come when watchmen will shout from the hill country of Ephraim, 'Come, let us go up to Jerusalem to worship the Lord our God.'"

Warriors

Isaiah 58:12 NLT

"Some of you will rebuild the deserted ruins of your cities. Then you will be known as a rebuilder of walls and a restorer of homes."

Prayer Point 2

- Pray that the Warriors (reformers) will arise from every sector in Nigeria and begin to rebuild the old waste places.

Isaiah 61:4 NLT

"They will rebuild the ancient ruins, repairing cities destroyed long ago. They will revive them, though they have been deserted for many generations."

Wasters

Proverbs 29:2, 16 NLT

"When the godly are in authority, the people rejoice. But when the wicked are in power, they groan.

When the wicked are in authority, sin flourishes, but the godly will live to see their downfall."

Prayer Point 3

- Pray for God to expose and dispose of those who waste Nigeria. Call for God's Hand of judgment to be heavy against them.
- Pray that the Lord will destroy their long standing covenant with hell especially their strong alliance with the spirit of corruption that has held our nation in bondage for so long.
- Pray that the Lord will take out the wicked that influence and speak to the throne of Nigeria and that the Lord scatters them with the blast of His nostrils.

Proverbs 25:5 NLT

"Remove the wicked from the king's court, and his reign will be made secure by justice."

Worried Ones

Isaiah 49:24-25 NLT

"Who can snatch the plunder of war from the hands of a warrior? Who can demand that a tyrant let his captives go? But the Lord says, "The captives of warriors will be released, and the plunder of tyrants will be retrieved. For I will fight those who fight you, and I will save your children."

Prayer Point 4

- Pray that the lawful captives and the prey of the terrible will receive their deliverance.

Jeremiah 31:11-12 NLT

"For the Lord has redeemed Israel from those too strong for them.

They will come home and sing songs of joy on the heights of Jerusalem.
They will be radiant because of the Lord's good gifts—the abundant crops of grain, new wine, and olive oil, and the healthy flocks and herds.
Their life will be like a watered garden, and all their sorrows will be gone."

Wise Ones

Proverbs 24:3-6 NLT

"A house is built by wisdom and becomes strong through good sense.
Through knowledge its rooms are filled with all sorts of precious riches and valuables.
The wise are mightier than the strong, and those with knowledge grow stronger and stronger.
So don't go to war without wise guidance; victory depends on having many advisers."

Prayer Point 5

- Pray that the wise ones of the kingdom will be multiplied in the land and they regain their place of influence in and around the throne of Nigeria.

Ecclesiastes 9:17-18 NLT

"Better to hear the quiet words of a wise person than the shouts of a foolish king.
Better to have wisdom than weapons of war, but one sinner can destroy much that is good."

2

BY MY SPIRIT SAYS THE LORD

CHAPTER TWO
PRAYER DAY 2

BY MY SPIRIT SAYS THE LORD

Prayer Quote

"The most important thing a born again Christian can do is to pray." Chuck Smith

True Intercessors sit where the people sit

Ezekiel 3:15 NLT

"Then I came to the colony of Judean exiles in Tel-abib, beside the Kebar River. I was overwhelmed and sat among them for seven days."

Ezekiel was AMONGST the captives, he sat where they sat and felt their pain.

This is just like Nehemiah who sat down and wept many days although he was in a faraway land in the palace.***(Nehemiah 1:4-11).***

True intercession always begins with being fully connected and loaded with the burden of what you are praying for. The lifting of that burden is the signal we receive from heaven that we have prayed through and have met heaven's righteous demand on the matter.

Prayer Point 1

- Let's pray for a genuine prayer burden from God to rest upon us through the duration of our prayers and not just an emotional burden that will lift after a few days.

Heaven's Perspective is Key

Ezekiel 1:1, 3 NLT

"On July 31 of my thirtieth year, while I was with the Judean exiles beside the Kebar River in Babylon, the heavens were opened and I saw visions of God (The Lord gave this message to Ezekiel son of Buzi, a priest, beside the Kebar River in the land of the Babylonians and he felt the hand of the Lord take hold of him.)"

Ezekiel had a spiritual revelation of the heavens opening and he saw visions of God, the Word of the Lord also came expressly and the hand of the Lord was upon him. Then he saw a revelation of He who sits on the Throne and was reminded of the unquestionable Sovereignty of God.

Clarity in what you see, hear and sense is of paramount importance in intercession. Although Ezekiel was sitting with others, he was the only one who saw the revelation. (True intercessors see heaven's perspective even when others don't).

Prayer Point 2

- Pray that we as intercessors will be reminded of the absolute sovereignty of God and be assured that our case is being presented to the highest authority of all.
- That no other authority can question, appeal or reverse what comes from this Throne.
- That no demonic entity or human government can alter what we receive from this Altar.
- Pray that we receive heaven's true perspective on present day Nigeria.
- You can go ahead and worship Him that sits upon the throne.

Spirit Led

Ezekiel 1:11-12, 20 NLT

"Each had two pairs of outstretched wings—one pair stretched out to touch the wings of the living beings on either side of it, and the other pair covered its body. They went in whatever direction the spirit chose, and they moved straight forward in any direction without turning around."

"The spirit of the living beings was in the wheels. So wherever the spirit went, the wheels and the living beings also went."

One of the outstanding features of the four living creatures Ezekiel saw was that they went wherever the Spirit wanted to go and were UNITED in their actions.

First of all the creatures didn't decide where to go but the Spirit of God did. Also note that they were prophetic because they anticipated where the Spirit wanted to go...and went WITH the Spirit. Not ahead or behind but they went WITH the Spirit.

Prayer Point 3

- Pray that we go wherever the Spirit of God leads us to go on this matter and pray we keep perfect timing with the Spirit of God.
- Pray that we act AS ONE...UNITED with the Holy Spirit and with each other ***(Psalms 133).***

Prompt Obedience

Ezekiel 1:14 NLT

"And the living beings darted to and fro like flashes of lightning."

The four living creatures also moved with lighting speed.
Immediate obedience to God's prompting is very critical.
He may prompt us to go left and in a flash prompt us to completely change direction.

Prayer Point 4

- Pray we act promptly to God's leading and that we stay ahead of the enemy in our spiritual warfare.

The Power of the Few

Ezekiel 1:24 NLT

"As they flew, their wings sounded to me like waves crashing against the shore or like the voice of the Almighty or like the shouting of a mighty army. When they stopped, they let down their wings."

Though they were only four creatures, their wings made sounds like the noise of many waters, like the voice of the Almighty and like the noise of an army.

Prayer Point 5

- Pray that though we may be few engaged in this intercessory prayer our effectiveness will be like that of a great army.

- That to the enemy we will be like the very voice of the Almighty that shakes the wilderness of Kadesh (**Psalms 29**).

3

DAY OF REPENTANCE

CHAPTER THREE
PRAYER DAY 3

DAY OF REPENTANCE

Prayer Quote

"Prayer is where the action is." John Wesley

If My People

2 Chronicles7:14

"If my people, who are called by my name, shall humble themselves, and pray, and seek my face, and turn from their wicked ways; then will I hear from heaven, and will forgive their sin, and will heal their land."

Today God demands of His people GENUINE REPENTANCE.
How dare we seek to STAND before The JUDGE of all the earth and demand for JUSTICE and JUDGMENT on behalf of an erring nation without first making sure our garments are TRULY WHITE?

Genesis 18:25b

"...shall not the judge of all the earth do right?"

Prayer Point 1

- Pray that we as God's people will approach His throne with a genuine heart of repentance.

Seek My Face

Nehemiah 1:4-9

"When I heard this, I sat down and wept. In fact, for days I mourned, fasted, and prayed to the God of heaven.

Then I said, "O Lord, God of heaven, the great and awesome God who keeps his covenant of unfailing love with those who love him and obey his commands, Listen to my prayer! Look down and see me praying night and day for your people Israel. I confess that we have sinned against you. Yes, even my own family and I have sinned!

We have sinned terribly by not obeying the commands, decrees, and regulations that you gave us through your servant Moses. "Please remember what you told your servant Moses: 'If you are unfaithful to me, I will scatter you among the nations. But if you return to me and obey my commands and live by them, then even if you are exiled to the ends of the earth, I will bring you back to the place I have chosen for my name to be honored."

Prayer Point 2

- Pray that as intercessors we will genuinely seek His face and not just His hands, and as we pray today our hearts shall connect with His heart's desire for our nation.

And Turn from their Wicked Ways

Zechariah 3:1-3

"And he shewed me Joshua the high priest standing before the angel of the Lord, and Satan standing at his right hand to resist him. And the Lord said

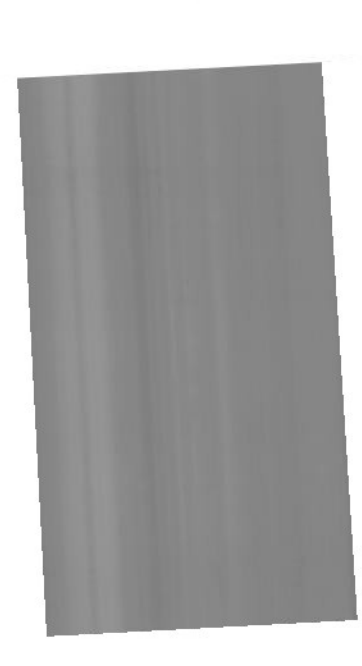

unto Satan, The LORD rebuke thee, O Satan; even the LORD that hath chosen Jerusalem rebuke thee: is not this a brand plucked out of the fire? Now Joshua was clothed with filthy garments, and stood before the angel."

How can a high priest STAND before God in filthy garments and expect heaven's intervention?
One word to describe this type of person is 'HYPOCRITE'. Little wonder why many prayers are not heard because all that noise amounts to a religious exercise in futility.
The enemy STOOD confidently by the right hand of the high priest to resist him because he had a strong case of ACCUSATION against him. So the high priest became speechless before God. How dare anyone approach God's Righteous Throne clad in FILTHY GARMENTS and expect to truly be heard?

Prayer Point 3

- Let's turn 180 degrees from all forms of wickedness. For there is nothing like small sins before Him with whom we have to do.

I will Hear from Heaven

Daniel 9:3
"So I turned to the Lord God and pleaded with him in prayer and fasting. I also wore rough burlap and sprinkled myself with ashes."

Prayer Point 4:

- Cry out to the LORD to hear us from His Holy dwelling place and no force in hell will be able to mute you.

I will Forgive their Sin

Daniel 9:19

"O Lord, hear. O Lord, forgive. O Lord, listen and act! For your own sake, do not delay, O my God, for your people and your city bear your name."

Prayer Point 5

- Thank Him that He has assured us of His forgiveness not because we deserved it but because He reserved it for us in Christ. Boldly declare that we have forgiveness through the blood of the Lamb. Appropriate the blood over our nation.

I will Heal their Land

Ezekiel 47:9

"And it shall be that every living thing that moves, wherever the rivers go, will live. There will be a very great multitude of fish, because these waters go there; for they will be healed, and everything will live wherever the river goes."

Prayer Point 6

- Pray earnestly for God to heal Nigeria and send His healing power to flow through every fabric of our nation. That His healing waters will flow as the River of God in Ezekiel 47 until every aspect gets flooded with God's healing river.

4

DIVINE JUDGMENT

CHAPTER FOUR
PRAYER DAY 4

DIVINE JUDGMENT

Prayer Quote

"God does nothing except in response to believing prayer." ***John Wesley*** *(Famous evangelist who spent 2 hours daily in prayer).*

Judgment upon Ungodly Heritage

Jeremiah 9:23-24 NLT

"This is what the Lord says: "Don't let the wise boast in their wisdom, or the powerful boast in their power, or the rich boast in their riches.
But those who wish to boast should boast in this alone: that they truly know me and understand that I am the Lord who demonstrates unfailing love and who brings justice and righteousness to the earth, and that I delight in these things. I, the Lord, have spoken"

King Ahab husband of the infamous Jezebel represents a line of leaders with an ungodly heritage who are sold out to wickedness (wasters) and had shed much innocent blood ***(1Kg16:29-33)***.

This warning cuts across the public and private sector, religious sector as well as leadership at all levels of society.

God is warning all leaders to stop getting carried away by the perks of their office and focus on the true burden and responsibility of leadership.

Many will not heed this warning as in the case of Ahab and will be judged accordingly but for the few that will heed this call God will show Himself merciful.

There will be a lot of replacements in the area of leadership but the question is this: 'Will the new and emerging leaders learn from the mistakes of their forebears?'

Prayer Point 1

- Declare that the Lord will NOT hold back His Hand of Judgment but that God will respond decisively to the cry of all the blood of the innocent they have shed just as He responded to the cry of the blood of Abel crying out for justice!

Genesis 4:9-11

"And the LORD said unto Cain, Where is Abel thy brother? And he said, I know not: Am I my brother's keeper?

And he said, What hast thou done? The voice of thy brother's blood crieth unto me from the ground

And now art thou cursed from the earth, which hath opened her mouth to receive thy brother's blood from thy hand;"

Prayerfully remove any false covering and confidence of the wicked that has made them to continue unabated in their evil and declare that they will be shaken and shattered from their very foundations.

Isaiah 28:17

"Judgment also will I lay to the line, and righteousness to the plummet: and the hail shall sweep away the refuge of lies, and the waters shall overflow the hiding place."

Pray that a new God fearing leadership shall arise in our land.

Obadiah 1:21

"And saviours shall come up on mount Zion to judge the mount of Esau; and the kingdom shall be the Lord's."

Judgment upon Jezebel daughter of Ethbaal (joined to Baal)

2 Kings 9:7-11

"And thou shalt smite the house of Ahab thy master, that I may avenge the blood of my servants the prophets, and the blood of all the servants of the Lord, at the hand of Jezebel.

For the whole house of Ahab shall perish: and I will cut off from Ahab him that pisseth against the wall, and him that is shut up and left in Israel:

And I will make the house of Ahab like the house of Jeroboam the son of Nebat, and like the house of Baasha the son of Ahijah:

And the dogs shall eat Jezebel in the portion of Jezreel, and there shall be none to bury her. And he opened the door, and fled.

Then Jehu came forth to the servants of his lord: and one said unto him, Is all well? Wherefore came this mad fellow to thee? And he said unto them, ye know the man, and his communication."

Jezebel represents those sold out to the spirit of witchcraft and divination and are influencing many leaders and causing them to perpetuate their evil. Jezebel was the daughter of Ethbaal and a priestess of Baal, she was a foreign wife who imported her gods when she married King Ahab. As a result she put the nation under a spell and made many to turn their backs on the God of Israel.

A Jezebel spirit runs a well-organized system of idolatry that influences every aspect of society.

Prayer Point 2

- Pray that Jezebel shall be judged like Ahab, the dogs will eat her flesh and lick her blood.

Judgment upon False Prophets

Psalms 9:16

"The Lord is known by the judgment which he executeth: the wicked is snared in the work of his own hands. Higgaion. Selah."

Jeremiah 29:21

"Thus saith the Lord of hosts, the God of Israel, of Ahab the son of Kolaiah, and of Zedekiah the son of Maaseiah, which prophesy a lie unto you in my name; Behold, I will deliver them into the hand of Nebuchadnezzar king of Babylon; and he shall slay them before your eyes;"

Zedekiah son of Chenaanah the false prophet was very showy and dramatic ***(1 Kings 22).***

Zedekiah (just like all false prophets and marabouts) kept telling Ahab what he WANTED to hear not what he NEEDED to hear, therefore reinforcing his wickedness rather than confronting it.

These false prophets are only concerned about being politically correct and maintaining a good self-image and are operating with a lying spirit.

Prayer Point 3

- Pray that God's hand of judgment will by no means spare these charlatans.

Other Scripture reference

Psalms 37:28-40

"For the Lord loveth judgment, and forsaketh not his saints; they are preserved for ever: but the seed of the wicked shall be cut off.
The righteous shall inherit the land, and dwell therein for ever.
The mouth of the righteous speaketh wisdom, and his tongue talketh of judgment.
The law of his God is in his heart; none of his steps shall slide.
The wicked watcheth the righteous, and seeketh to slay him.
The Lord will not leave him in his hand, nor condemn him when he is judged.
Wait on the Lord, and keep his way, and he shall exalt thee to inherit the land: when the wicked are cut off, thou shalt see it.
I have seen the wicked in great power, and spreading himself like a green bay tree.
Yet he passed away, and, lo, he was not: yea, I sought him, but he could not be found.
Mark the perfect man, and behold the upright: for the end of that man is peace.
But the transgressors shall be destroyed together: the end of the wicked shall be cut off.
But the salvation of the righteous is of the Lord: he is their strength in the time of trouble.
And the Lord shall help them, and deliver them: he shall deliver them from the wicked, and save them, because they trust in him."

5

OUR NATIONAL IDEOLOGY - THE NIGERIAN DREAM

CHAPTER FIVE
PRAYER DAY 5

OUR NATIONAL IDEOLOGY - THE NIGERIAN DREAM

Prayer Quote

"Talking to men for God is a great thing, but talking to God for men is greater still." E.M. Bounds

Time to Build

Ecclesiastes 3:1-3 NLT

"For everything there is a season, a time for every activity under heaven.
A time to be born and a time to die. A time to plant and a time to harvest.
A time to kill and a time to heal. A time to tear down and a time to build up."

The above scripture clearly states that there is a time and season for EVERY purpose under heaven.

My heart is heavy, my spirit burdened with the plight of our people. As I write I feel a holy indignation about the sad state of our dear STATE.

When will this end? When will we come into our promised land? When will OUR DREAM finally come true? When will our story of gloom be turned to our story of glory?

Come to think of it what really is THE NIGERIAN DREAM? We have seen nations make the transition from third world to first...so when will our OWN transition happen? What is our clearly defined national ideology?

That means that since NIGERIA is under heaven, we must have our set TIME and SEASON. Of all the things listed in the above scripture we as a people have experienced all but the last one. THE TIME TO BUILD UP.

How many of us are flying the national flag in our homes, on our cars or in our hearts? How many are really and truly proudly Nigerian? To put it in context, How many are truly proud of our leaders?

How many are genuinely proud of our law enforcement agents and agencies: customs, immigration, police force, etc?

How many are proud of using generators more than Power Holding Company of Nigeria (PHCN)?

How many are proud of the unending baton exchange between malaria and typhoid in their households?

How many are proud of the roads, health care, education system? The average Nigerian has had enough and yearns for change.

We yearn for a national ideology that is clear, precise and practicable.

Prayer Point 1

- Ask the Lord to give us His blueprint for our national ideology. That He will stir our hearts to seek and clearly define our national aspiration and ideology as a people. That we will not be visionless people led by visionless leaders but a people with shared values, a common vision and a common destiny.

Proverbs 29:18

"Where there is no vision, the people perish: but he that keepeth the law, happy is he."

Let the Reformers Arise

Nehemiah 2:17-20

"Then said I unto them, ye see the distress that we are in, how Jerusalem lieth waste, and the gates thereof are burned with fire: come, and let us build up the wall of Jerusalem, that we be no more a reproach.

Then I told them of the hand of my God which was good upon me; as also the king's words that he had spoken unto me. And they said, Let us rise up and build. So they strengthened their hands for this good work.

But when Sanballat the Horonite, and Tobiah the servant, the Ammonite, and Geshem the Arabian, heard it, they laughed us to scorn, and despised us, and said, what is this thing that ye do? Will ye rebel against the king?

Then answered I them, and said unto them, The God of heaven, he will prosper us; therefore we his servants will arise and build: but ye have no portion, nor right, nor memorial, in Jerusalem."

It's time for warriors and reformers to arise and rebuild our beloved country

Prayer Point 2

- Ask the Lord to strengthen every Nehemiah that seeks to rebuild our great nation and to frustrate every Sanballat, Tobiah and Geshem that seeks to divide us.

Time to Write and Do

Habakkuk 2:1-3

"I will stand upon my watch, and set me upon the tower, and will watch to see what he will say unto me, and what I shall answer when I am reproved. And the Lord answered me, and said, write the vision, and make it plain upon tables, that he may run that readeth it. For the vision is yet for an appointed time, but at the end it shall speak, and not lie: though it tarry, wait for it; because it will surely come, it will not tarry."

Every watchman must be armed with a pen to write what the Lord reveals in their prayer place.

I believe for most of you holding this book, it's not just a coincidence or a mere desire to satisfy a religious itch....but it was occasioned by God to turn you into a WARRIOR/REFORMER (refer to previous explanation on the 5 kinds of Nigerians).

I am fully persuaded that the time has come. The time to articulate a national ideology. The time to demand of our leaders...'deliver or depart'. The time for the long arm of justice to begin to take hold and recover what is rightfully ours. The time to be resolute, civil but persistent until positive CHANGE happens.

So as we pray and act in our own little way...I would like to strongly recommend that you draw out about 5 to 7 point manifesto that clearly states our NATIONAL IDEOLOGY and our NATIONAL ASPIRATIONS. Most national ideologies have two dimensions:

Goals: How society should work.

Methods: The most appropriate way to achieve the ideal arrangement.

Start by focusing on the first part - *Goals*. (The Methods will require a more engaging time of national dialogue and debate that may take a few months). What are those things that we should expect of our Nation, our leaders and ourselves? Those things that cannot be compromised that will make us all

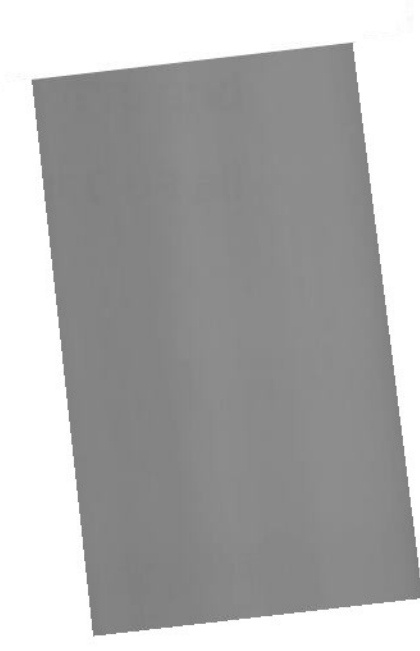

proudly Nigerian. Those things that will give our children hope for a better tomorrow, that will give us all a true sense patriotism and belonging. Those things that will become the heartbeat of every Nigerian. Those things that we will all proudly talk about, sing about, write about and go about fulfilling without any sense of being disenfranchised. Those things that our future generations will bless us for putting in place.

The SINGAPORE Example. The Singapore National Ideology called the Singapore's Shared Values was passed into law in 15 Jan 1991. The basis for developing this Singapore identity was to identify key common values that all racial groups and faiths can subscribe to and live by. Outside of these Shared Values, each community can practise its own values as long as they are not in conflict with national ones. The main theme underlying the set of Shared Values emphasises communitarian values and reflects Singapore's heritage.

The Five Statements of the Singapore Shared Values can be seen in the National Library Board(NLB) website of Singapore: (NATIONAL LIBRARY BOARD OF SINGAPORE, 2004).[4]

Prayer Point 3

- Take some time and pray about this very important issue.

Then fully write down what you strongly believe should be our common goals as a people, those things EVERY Nigerian should aspire for? These goals must be all inclusive irrespective of gender, tribe, religion or economic standing. Kindly feel free to share it with your family, friends, colleagues, social media contacts and every Nigerian in your sphere of influence. You can also send it to my contact details given in this book.

Do it because you love Nigeria, do it because you believe in God's promise over her.

God bless you as you PRAY and ACT right.

6

GETTING RID OF GRASSHOPPER MENTALITY

CHAPTER SIX
PRAYER DAY 6

Prayer Quote

"If the church wants a better pastor, it only needs to pray for the one it has." Anonymous

Wasted Generation

Matthew 23:37-38

"O Jerusalem, Jerusalem, thou that killest the prophets, and stonest them which are sent unto thee, how often would I have gathered thy children together, even as a hen gathereth her chickens under her wings, and ye would not!

Behold, your house is left unto you desolate."

This text clearly tells us that it is possible to miss one's moment. Not only that, but a whole generation can actually miss their moment.

A clear example of that is in the account of the Israelites in the wilderness.

Numbers 14:27-31

"How long shall I bear with this evil congregation, which murmur against me? I have heard the murmurings of the children of Israel, which they murmur against me.

Say unto them, as truly as I live, saith the Lord, as ye have spoken in mine ears, so will I do to you:

Your carcases shall fall in this wilderness; and all that were numbered of you, according to your whole number, from twenty years old and upward,

which have murmured against me,
Doubtless ye shall not come into the land, concerning which I sware to make you dwell therein, save Caleb the son of Jephunneh, and Joshua the son of Nun.
But your little ones, which ye said should be a prey, them will I bring in, and they shall know the land which ye have despised."

This means God originally intended for all the Israelites to enter the Promised Land but due to their OWN doing, all those who were age 20 and up MISSED OUT. That whole generation missed their moment EXCEPT Joshua and Caleb....all others became part of a WASTED GENERATION.

Prayer Point 1

- Pray that our generation will not miss her moment that we will not miss the time of our visitation. That we will not be a wasted generation.
- Pray that we as a people in this moment in history will take responsibility and rise from the dust and loose ourselves from the snare that binds us.

Isaiah 52:2

"Shake thyself from the dust; arise, and sit down, O Jerusalem: loose thyself from the bands of thy neck, O captive daughter of Zion."

Getting rid of the Grasshopper Mentality

Numbers 13:30-33

"And Caleb stilled the people before Moses, and said, Let us go up at once, and possess it; for we are well able to overcome it.
But the men that went up with him said, We be not able to go up against the

people; for they are stronger than we.
And they brought up an evil report of the land which they had searched unto the children of Israel, saying, The land, through which we have gone to search it, is a land that eateth up the inhabitants thereof; and all the people that we saw in it are men of a great stature.
And there we saw the giants, the sons of Anak, which come of the giants: and we were in our own sight as grasshoppers, and so we were in their sight."

Numbers 14:1-24
"And all the congregation lifted up their voice, and cried; and the people wept that night.
And all the children of Israel murmured against Moses and against Aaron: and the whole congregation said unto them, Would God that we had died in the land of Egypt! Or would God we had died in this wilderness! "

The twelve spies were all leaders from their respective tribes so their actions had great repercussions not only on themselves but also upon all those they were leading.
Sadly speaking, the mindset of the 10 spies (Leaders) was the mindset of the majority of the people. And since the 10 spies(Leaders) couldn't see their way into the promised Land, the majority of the congregation followed suit and murmured against the Lord because they simply could not rise beyond the 'small mindedness' of their leaders.
Let's not assume for one moment that we can get past the mindset of those who lead us. Little wonder we find that the same mindset of a waster in the highest level of leadership is being replicated at the lowest level of leadership.

We speak of corruption amongst highly placed politicians but we find the same in our schools....when some of our lecturers are demanding bribes either in cash or kind from our future leaders before they can 'obtain' their 'good' degrees.

These leaders of tomorrow are actually being schooled unwittingly to perpetuate the pathetic pattern we all are crying out against today.

This problem has eaten deeply into every fabric of our nation, that it is now a 'CULTURE OF LAWLESSNESS' from driving against traffic, jumping queues, throwing refuse on the roads, building mansions on sewage drains, 'settling' the police officer because of questionable papers, etc

This I regard as a 'GRASSHOPPER MENTALITY'.

Can someone explain why we hero worship those with questionable wealth and completely ignore or even vilify men and women of integrity and sound wisdom who are not wealthy?

Why do we celebrate the governor and neglect the primary school teacher. Is it mere coincidence or are there contracts in mind? Most of us have never gone back to our primary school teacher with a thank you note but we have taken several notes to the governor for personal favors that most times have been turned down.

Can someone explain why we 'spray' naira and even foreign currencies at our weddings when billionaires in developed countries don't? Why we spend so much to buy things from oversees that are not acclimatized to our tropical weather rather than just developing what works for us?

Why are we such a consumer nation? Is the problem really just because of bad leadership or something in our psyche? These are just a few of the SOCIETAL SUICIDE we are committing that are 'killing us softly' as a nation.

Nigerians have a way of creating jokes out of everything...we are so fun

loving that we don't seem to deal with the challenges we are facing with the seriousness it deserves. For example some time ago someone posted the following:

"ASUU Strike started Dec 4
Fuel Subsidy started Jan 1
NLC Strike Started Jan 9
May God deliver Naija from 419."

Kindly forgive me but I no longer find these jokes funny.

Let's use our creative minds to proffer a way out of this wilderness instead of creating jokes out of our crisis. Can you tell me how many jokes Jesus cracked in the bible? I'm not saying jokes are bad, of course some laughter is good for the soul but THIS IS NOT THE TIME FOR JOKES.
The destiny of our nation and future generations of Nigerians are hanging in the balance. Just imagine Queen Esther joking when Mordecai sent her the message of the planned alienation of her countrymen by Haman. In fact her little protest was met by a stern rebuke that jolted her back to reality until she declared those famous words: 'IF I PERISH, I PERISH'

Esther 4:13-16
"Then Mordecai commanded to answer Esther, Think not with thyself that thou shalt escape in the king's house, more than all the Jews. For if thou altogether holdest thy peace at this time, then shall there enlargement and deliverance arise to the Jews from another place; but thou and thy father's house shall be destroyed: and who knoweth whether thou art come to the kingdom for such a time as this? Then Esther bade them return Mordecai this answer, Go, gather together all the Jews that are present in Shushan,

and fast ye for me, and neither eat nor drink three days, night or day: I also and my maidens will fast likewise; and so will I go in unto the king, which is not according to the law: and if I perish, I perish."

Prayer Point 2

- Pray that God rid us of the 'small mindedness' and 'Grasshopper Mentality' that has made our society so under-developed despite our intellectual prowess and great wealth potential as a people.(For those leading us are not aliens from another planet but they are a BIGGER reflection of what we are) Sad but true.
- Let's not only pray but let's also commit to a mind renewal that will not only equip us, but also empower us to be all God wants us to be as a people and to DO all we have to do to make the change.
- That we will all be willing to make the necessary sacrifices to achieve the desired outcome.

We shall not be denied

Hebrews 3:12-19

"Take heed, brethren, lest there be in any of you an evil heart of unbelief, in departing from the living God.

But exhort one another daily, while it is called to day; lest any of you be hardened through the deceitfulness of sin.

For we are made partakers of Christ, if we hold the beginning of our confidence steadfast unto the end;

While it is said, today if ye will hear his voice, harden not your hearts, as in the provocation. For some, when they had heard, did provoke: howbeit not all that came out of Egypt by Moses.

But with whom was he grieved forty years? Was it not with them that had sinned, whose carcases fell in the wilderness?
And to whom sware he that they should not enter into his rest, but to them that believed not?
We see that they could not enter in because of unbelief."

Due to the evil report of ten spies two things happened:
Promise Denied. The ten spies and all those age 20 and above didn't enter the Promised Land except Joshua and Caleb. That generation was DENIED what God had promised them because they did not believe.
Promise Delayed. Though Joshua and Caleb entered the Promised Land they suffered a 40 year DELAY because of the evil report of the other spies. This means that we have to jealously guard our close associations because the wrong company can DELAY the fulfilment of a sure word of prophecy over a person's life.

Proverbs 13:20
"He that walketh with wise men shall be wise: but a companion of fools shall be destroyed."

Prayer Point 3
- Pray that we will not be delayed, neither will we be denied that which God has for us as a people.
- That God will help us to begin a conversation with people of like minds like Joshua and Caleb until our voices ring loud and clear. Until judgment runs down as waters and righteous as a mighty stream.

Amos 5:24

"But let judgment run down as waters, and righteousness as a mighty stream."

7

CARPENTERS OF HIS NOBLE ARMY

CHAPTER SEVEN
PRAYER DAY 7

CARPENTERS OF HIS NOBLE ARMY

Prayer Quote

"Seven days without prayer makes one weak." Allen E. Vartlett

The Four Horns

Zechariah 1:18-21

"Then lifted I up mine eyes, and saw, and behold four horns. And I said unto the angel that talked with me, What be these? And he answered me, These are the horns which have scattered Judah, Israel, and Jerusalem. And the Lord shewed me four carpenters. Then said I, What come these to do? And he spake, saying, These are the horns which have scattered Judah, so that no man did lift up his head: but these are come to fray them, to cast out the horns of the Gentiles, which lifted up their horn over the land of Judah to scatter it."

Notice only four horns scattered the nation, only a relatively few are behind the pathetic predicament of our nation.

Prayer Point 1

- Ask the Lord to expose the specific horns behind the culture of corruption in Nigeria. That He will expose all their vast structures and networks both local and foreign

Carpenters Of His Noble Army(COHNA)

2 Kings 9:4-7

"So the young man, even the young man the prophet, went to Ramothgilead. And when he came, behold, the captains of the host were sitting; and he said, I have an errand to thee, O captain. And Jehu said, Unto which of all us? And he said, To thee, O captain. And he arose, and went into the house; and he poured the oil on his head, and said unto him, Thus saith the Lord God of Israel, I have anointed thee king over the people of the LORD, even over Israel. And thou shalt smite the house of Ahab thy master, that I may avenge the blood of my servants the prophets, and the blood of all the servants of the Lord, at the hand of Jezebel."

2 Kings 9:30-33

"And when Jehu was come to Jezreel, Jezebel heard of it; and she painted her face, and tired her head, and looked out at a window.
And as Jehu entered in at the gate, she said, Had Zimri peace, who slew his master?
And he lifted up his face to the window, and said, Who is on my side? who? And there looked out to him two or three eunuchs.
And he said, Throw her down. So they threw her down: and some of her blood was sprinkled on the wall, and on the horses: and he trode her under foot."

God had to raise an elite corps of carpenters....one I call Carpenters Of His Noble Army (COHNA). These 'Warrior' carpenters knew what many didn't know....you have to be a specialist in order to fulfill your purpose....beating about the bush and being a jack of all trades usually never delivers at the end of the day.

This should make us realise that the special challenges we face as a people will require people with unique skills and understanding-especially in the spirit in order to tackle the few horns that are scattering our country.

From all indications these horns or cabals (Wasters) are still firmly secure but their covenant with hell shall be disannulled.

Prayer Point 2

- Ask the Lord at this time to anoint and raise His carpenters to tackle the horns scattering Nigeria.
- Ask the Lord that through the prayer efforts of His Noble Carpenters that He will raise a JEHU COMPANY that will be a non compromising group of REFORMERS who will not be compromised in anyway by Jezebel but will execute justice and judgment upon all to whom it is due.

Fraying every Spiritual Horn of the Enemy

Ezekiel 21:27

"I will overturn, overturn, overturn, it: and it shall be no more, until he come whose right it is; and I will give it him. Every blessing."

These carpenters had to FRAY the horns, not cut them for they knew that the only permanent solution to dealing with the notorious horns was to GRIND THEM TO POWDER.

GRINDING OR FRAYING the horns takes time, perseverance and dogged commitment to your mission.

This tells us of the importance of long term strategies rather than a short term 'fire brigade' approaches to spiritual warfare.

Prayer Point 3

- Pray that God will give every watchman and reformer the patience and commitment to engage in long Strategic Warfare until victory is achieved.

WEEK TWO

SECOND PROPHECY ON NIGERIA: S.P.E.A.R.H.E.A.D. (RECEIVED 2017)

BACKGROUND

No Justice

The Lord started by saying that prophetically Nigeria has been largely in Isaiah 59.

Isaiah 59:1-3 (NLT)
"Listen! The Lord's arm is not too weak to save you, nor is his ear too deaf to hear you call.
It's your sins that have cut you off from God. Because of your sins, he has turned away and will not listen anymore.
Your hands are the hands of murderers, and your fingers are filthy with sin. Your lips are full of lies, and your mouth spews corruption."

The reason it seems the Lord has not been listening to the cry of well-meaning Nigerians (Watchmen) is because for too long the 'wasters' have been in charge of the affairs of the Land.

Isaiah 59:4-8
"No one cares about being fair and honest. The people's lawsuits are based on lies. They conceive evil deeds and then give birth to sin.
They hatch deadly snakes and weave spiders' webs. Whoever eats their

eggs will die; whoever cracks them will hatch a viper.
Their webs can't be made into clothing, and nothing they do is productive.
All their activity is filled with sin, and violence is their trademark.
Their feet run to do evil, and they rush to commit murder. They think only about sinning. Misery and destruction always follow them.
They don't know where to find peace or what it means to be just and good.
They have mapped out crooked roads, and no one who follows them knows a moment's peace."

The efforts of the Watchmen, Warriors and Wise Ones have been too weak as the Wasters are having their way in oppressing the Worried Ones and ruling in every sphere of society (Executive, Legislative, Judiciary, Religious etc).

Isaiah 59:9-14

"So there is no justice among us, and we know nothing about right living. We look for light but find only darkness. We look for bright skies but walk in gloom.
We grope like the blind along a wall, feeling our way like people without eyes. Even at brightest noontime, we stumble as though it were dark. Among the living, we are like the dead.
We growl like hungry bears; we moan like mournful doves.
We look for justice, but it never comes. We look for rescue, but it is far away from us.
For our sins are piled up before God and testify against us. Yes, we know what sinners we are.
We know we have rebelled and have denied the Lord. We have turned our backs on our God. We know how unfair and oppressive we have been,

carefully planning our deceitful lies.
Our courts oppose the righteous, and justice is nowhere to be found. Truth stumbles in the streets, and honesty has been outlawed."

The State has been in a very sad state for just too long. Justice is Missing in Action (MIA), while oppression and corruption are in the nation's every institution.

Isaiah 59:15-19

"Yes, truth is gone, and anyone who renounces evil is attacked. The Lord looked and was displeased to find there was no justice. He was amazed to see that no one intervened to help the oppressed. So he himself stepped in to save them with his strong arm, and his justice sustained him.
He put on righteousness as his body armor, and placed the helmet of salvation on his head. He clothed himself with a robe of vengeance and wrapped himself in a cloak of divine passion.
He will repay his enemies for their evil deeds. His fury will fall on his foes. He will pay them back even to the ends of the earth.
In the west, people will respect the name of the Lord; in the east, they will glorify him. For he will come like a raging flood tide driven by the breath of the Lord."

It's been a hopeless case for decades but for Our God who is now stepping into the Arena. He has an undying love for Nigeria and will show Himself strong.

Isaiah 59:20-21
"The Redeemer will come to Jerusalem to buy back those in Israel who have turned from their sins," says the Lord.
"And this is my covenant with them," says the Lord. "My Spirit will not leave them, and neither will these words I have given you. They will be on your lips and on the lips of your children and your children's children forever. I, the Lord, have spoken!"

This intervention is because there is a divine promise over Nigeria and she has within her a few that the Lord regards greatly...yes her company of Watchmen, Warriors and Wise Ones, her Noahs, Daniels, and Jobs. A minority group but they matter extremely to heaven.

PROPHECY: SEVEN NIGERIAN CITIES WILL S.P.E.A.R.H.E.A.D. THE NATION'S PROPHETIC TRANSFORMATION

In this prophecy the Lord told me He will S.P.E.A.R.H.E.A.D. the transformation of Nigeria according to the last 7 chapters of Isaiah. Prophetically Nigeria has been largely in Isaiah 59 (No Justice). In 7 years from today (Sunday 3 September 2017) God is going to wipe away the power of Amalek (Amalek stands for an overwhemly stubborn and relentless enemy that takes advantage of the weak) and He will bring about a transformation in line with the last 7 chapters of Isaiah.

Isaiah 60 - Gathering begins
Isaiah 61 - Repairers strategize for rebuilding
Isaiah 62 - Watchmen role fully restored

Isaiah 63 - Day of vengeance & year of redemption

Isaiah 64 - Nations tremble at God's mountain melting presence

Isaiah 65 - Spiritual cleansing as false prophets & altars completely give way to the true

Isaiah 66 - A new nation is born at once

God will raise 7 significant cities in Nigeria where His altar will be the predominant altar to S.P.E.A.R.H.E.A.D. this prophetic transformation.

S - Seek God's face intensely

P - Pray for His Kingdom to come and His will to be done

E - Engage with the spiritual darkness (Amalekites) over the land.

A - Agree with heaven (As Joshua & Moses did)

R - Root out the foundations of evil

H - Hold up their hands till victory is won.

E - Establish righteousness that will exalt Nigeria to heights never reached before

A - Align Nigeria and Africa to God's end time Agenda

D - Deliver the Dominion of Nigeria over the nations.

God has sent the angel of His presence to support the prince over Nigeria and the angels assigned over these 7 cities to dislodge the princes of darkness over these cities.

Each city will have 7 leading churches (49 churches) who will collaborate with the Heavenly forces, in each church at least 7 leading warriors (*343 special warriors) who will War for the next 7 years with Amalek till the Amalekites are discomfited (defeat utterly, rout out).

Kindly note that the total numbers of warring intercessors indicated are minimum number not maximum.

These warriors shall spiritually lift up the SPEARHEAD of God's deliverance like Joshua did over Ai until victory is fully secured.

Joshua 8:18-19, 26

"Then the Lord said to Joshua, "Stretch out the spear that is in your hand toward Ai, for I will give it into your hand." And Joshua stretched out the spear that was in his hand toward the city.

So those in ambush arose quickly out of their place; they ran as soon as he had stretched out his hand, and they entered the city and took it, and hurried to set the city on fire.

For Joshua did not draw back his hand, with which he stretched out the spear, until he had utterly destroyed all the inhabitants of Ai."

The author in October 2019 prayerfully identified what he perceived to be the seven states in Nigeria that will be the arrowheads for the revival.

These seven states and governing centres are located in the 6 geopolitical zones of Nigeria and Federal Capital Territory (FCT) as follows:

A	-	Abuja	-	FCT
R	-	Rivers	-	South South
K	-	Kaduna	-	North West
P	-	Plateau	-	North Central
L	-	Lagos	-	South west
E	-	Enugu	-	South East
A	-	Adamawa	-	North East

These cities are only catalyst cities as the prayer revival will not be limited to them only.

Great and unstoppable waves of God's power and glory shall issue forth from these cities.

8

THE GATHERING BEGINS

CHAPTER EIGHT
PRAYER DAY 8

THE GATHERING BEGINS

Prayer Quote

"Satan does not care how many people read about prayer if only he can keep them from praying". Paul E. Billheimer

Future Glory for Nigeria

Isaiah 60:1-3 (NLT)

"Arise, Jerusalem! Let your light shine for all to see. For the glory of the Lord rises to shine on you.

Darkness as black as night covers all the nations of the earth, but the glory of the Lord rises and appears over you.

All nations will come to your light; mighty kings will come to see your radiance."

In Scripture, prophetic promises like this one have multiple applications. Although it primarily speaks into the future about the New Jerusalem, it has been quickened and can be applied to Nigeria's future glory. As things are going from bad to worse in the world scene, the Lord has chosen Nigeria as one of the beacons of hope in these last days.

This is a personal prophecy over a nation and so it's a 'conditional prophecy' and just like all personal prophecies over a people, a family or an individual...certain conditions must be met to see them fulfilled in a generation.

Prayer Point 1

- Pray that as Nigerians we will recognize God's prophetic hand upon us and begin to align ourselves to see the hand of God move us from oppression to His glorious expression for our nation.

Nigerians in Diaspora will Remember Home

Isaiah 60:4-11 (NLT)

"Look and see, for everyone is coming home! Your sons are coming from distant lands; your little daughters will be carried home.

Your eyes will shine, and your heart will thrill with joy, for merchants from around the world will come to you. They will bring you the wealth of many lands.

Vast caravans of camels will converge on you, the camels of Midian and Ephah. The people of Sheba will bring gold and frankincense and will come worshiping the Lord.

The flocks of Kedar will be given to you, and the rams of Nebaioth will be brought for my altars. I will accept their offerings, and I will make my Temple glorious.

"And what do I see flying like clouds to Israel, like doves to their nests?

They are ships from the ends of the earth, from lands that trust in me, led by the great ships of Tarshish. They are bringing the people of Israel home from far away, carrying their silver and gold. They will honor the Lord your God, the Holy One of Israel, for he has filled you with splendor.

"Foreigners will come to rebuild your towns, and their kings will serve you. For though I have destroyed you in my anger, I will now have mercy on you through my grace.

Your gates will stay open day and night to receive the wealth of many lands.

The kings of the world will be led as captives in a victory procession."

The time will come when many in diaspora will return home and many who are still abroad will start looking homeward to make their contribution. Also many foreign nations will invest in Nigeria.

Prayer Point 2

- Pray for the stirring of the hearts of Nigerians in the diaspora for homeward migration and investments. That there will be an enabling environment for Foreign Direct Investments, massive developments and a conducive atmosphere for industrialisation to thrive.

God will make His Church in Nigeria Glorious

Isaiah 60:12-13

"For the nations that refuse to serve you will be destroyed. "The glory of Lebanon will be yours—the forests of cypress, fir, and pine—to beautify my sanctuary." My Temple will be glorious!"

God will judge any foreign induced hindrances to Nigeria's unity, peace, progress and prosperity.
The Lord will beautify His church in Nigeria.

Prayer Point 3

- Pronounce God's judgment upon any nation that is committed to keeping Nigeria down on her back.
- Declare that the nation is rising and no foreign power shall hinder her because it's her time.

- Call forth the church in Nigeria to Arise and Shine for her light has come.

Reverse emigration - The World comes to Nigeria

Isaiah 60:14-6

"The descendants of your tormentors will come and bow before you. Those who despised you will kiss your feet. They will call you the City of the Lord, and Zion of the Holy One of Israel. "Though you were once despised and hated, with no one traveling through you, I will make you beautiful forever, a joy to all generations.

Powerful kings and mighty nations will satisfy your every need, as though you were a child nursing at the breast of a queen.

You will know at last that I, the Lord, am your Saviour and your Redeemer, the Mighty One of Israel."

Those who previously and relentlessly exploited the nation shall count it an honor to be associated with Nigeria in the future.

Many world leaders and many tourists shall flow into the nation and serve the interest of Nigeria continually.

Prayer Point 4

- Pray that the descendants of those who once milked Nigeria shall serve milk and honey to the land they once oppressed. Call forth powerful world leaders to serve the interest of Nigeria.

Development shall thrive and internal unrest shall cease

Isaiah 60: 17-22

"I will exchange your bronze for gold, your iron for silver, your wood for bronze, and your stones for iron. I will make peace your leader and righteousness your ruler.

Violence will disappear from your land; the desolation and destruction of war will end.

Salvation will surround you like city walls, and praise will be on the lips of all who enter there.

"No longer will you need the sun to shine by day, nor the moon to give its light by night, for the Lord your God will be your everlasting light, and your God will be your glory.

Your sun will never set; your moon will not go down.

For the Lord will be your everlasting light

Your days of mourning will come to an end .All your people will be righteous.

They will possess their land forever, for I will plant them there with my own hands in order to bring myself glory

The smallest family will become a thousand people, and the tiniest group will become a mighty nation.

At the right time, I, the Lord, will make it happen."

The comparative advantage of Nigeria will start to show forth amongst the nations.

The *entrepreneurial spirit* of Nigerians shall attract world attention and bring a whole new level of development to the nation.

Agitations for cessation shall cease as there will be equitable distribution of wealth across all geopolitical zones.

Prayer Point 5

- Pray that the "sun" of development and national renaissance over Nigeria shall never set. Rebuke the company of spearmen that delight in civil unrest and speak peace to all parts of the country.

9

REPAIRERS STRATEGIZE FOR REBUILDING

CHAPTER NINE
PRAYER DAY 9

REPAIRERS STRATEGIZE FOR REBUILDING

Prayer Quote

"Men may spurn our appeals, reject our message, oppose our arguments, despise our persons, but they are helpless against our prayers." Sidlow Baxter

Good News for the Oppressed (Worried Ones)

Isaiah 61:1-3 (NLT)

The Spirit of the Sovereign Lord is upon me, for the Lord has anointed me to bring good news to the poor.

He has sent me to comfort the broken-hearted and to proclaim that captives will be released and prisoners will be freed.

He has sent me to tell those who mourn that the time of the Lord's favor has come, and with it, the day of God's anger against their enemies.

To all who mourn in Israel, he will give a crown of beauty for ashes, a joyous blessing instead of mourning, festive praise instead of despair.

In their righteousness, they will be like great oaks that the Lord has planted for his own glory."

There will be a sovereign move of the Spirit of God across the land to set the captives free. It will be a season of good news in the nation as the upset ones will become the set up ones and princes in their father land.

Prayer Point 1

- Ask for a powerful move of the Spirit of God and for the avalanche of His glory to sweep across Nigeria as never before. That there will be an exchange of beauty for ashes, of joyous blessing for mourning and festive praise instead of despair.

National Reformers (Warriors) shall rise

Isaiah 61: 4

"They will rebuild the ancient ruins, repairing cities destroyed long ago. They will revive them, though they have been deserted for many generations."

A whole new generation of reformers and national transformers shall arise in every sector of the nation.

Prayer Point 2

- Pray that our youths (new generation of reformers) shall arise and rebuild the old waste places and repair the damages caused by previous generation of Wasters.

Double Honor

Isaiah 61:5-7

"Foreigners will be your servants. They will feed your flocks and plow your fields and tend your vineyards.

You will be called priests of the Lord, ministers of our God.

You will feed on the treasures of the nations and boast in their riches. Instead of shame and dishonor you will enjoy a double share of honor. You will possess a double portion of prosperity in your land, and everlasting joy will be yours."

Nigeria shall reap a mighty harvest of foreigners deploying their expertise in the country because she had sown through the labors of her sons and daughters who had lent their talents abroad for so many years.
The nation shall enjoy double honor and shed away the stench of shameful reputation she had endured in the past.

Prayer Point 3

- Pray for an inflow of foreign expertise in specific industries and areas of society to equip Nigerians with the most needed skills. That Nigeria will feed from the abundance and treasures of the nations. Declare that we as a people have come into our time of double honor and double portion prosperity.

Peace and Justice shall reign

Isaiah 61: 8-9

"For I, the Lord, love justice. I hate robbery and wrongdoing. I will faithfully reward my people for their suffering and make an everlasting covenant with them.
Their descendants will be recognized and honored among the nations.
Everyone will realize that they are a people the Lord has blessed."

Justice shall reign from one end of the nation to the other.

Nigerians shall be held in high honor all over the world.

Prayer Point 4

Second stanza of our national anthem

- Oh God of creation,
- Direct our noble cause
- Guide our leaders right
- Help our youths the truth to know
- In love and honesty to grow
- And living just and true
- Great lofty heights attain
- To build a nation where peace and justice shall reign.

"Oh God of creation"

Let us acknowledge that God is the creator of Nigeria.

Re-state and reinforce (in the spirit) His lordship over Nigeria. Pray in the spirit.

Acts 17:26

"From one man he made every nation of men that they should inhabit the whole earth; and he determined the times set for them and the exact places where they should live"

"Direct our noble cause"

Pray for His directions in the affairs of our country

"Guide our leaders right"

Pray that he will "guide our leaders right" and those that refuse to be guided right be removed immediately.

"Help our youths the truth to know"

Pray for our youths to know the truth.

That a holy anger will rise up in them such that they will not be satisfied with the mediocrity and wickedness we see today.

That they will not be willing or even unwilling vehicles of retrogression

"In love and honesty to grow"

Here in this anthem we see some of our national values: unity, love, honesty, truth and justice.

Pray that love and honesty will be restored to our land and we will grow.

"And living just and true"

That truth and justice will reign.

"Great lofty heights attain"

Pray that we shall attain great lofty heights.

As watchmen our vision must include "lofty heights". List your lofty visions for Nigeria and pray over them. Be sure to include a vision of a Nigeria that will NOT continue to devour its best and promote its worst as obtains currently.

"To build a nation where peace and justice shall reign."

Pray that peace and justice shall reign in our nation.

Let's pray that divinely inspired love for Nigeria will fill its people at home and in Diaspora.

Pray for yourself and for all that are in position to make a difference, that we will be as patriotic as our national anthem and national pledge express.

Declare that Nigeria is a nation whose God is the Lord.

Psalms 33:12

"Blessed is the nation whose God is the Lord, The people He has chosen as His own inheritance."

Overwhelming Joy

Isaiah 61:10-11

"I am overwhelmed with joy in the Lord my God!

For he has dressed me with the clothing of salvation and draped me in a robe of righteousness.

I am like a bridegroom dressed for his wedding or a bride with her jewels.

The Sovereign Lord will show his justice to the nations of the world.

Everyone will praise him!

His righteousness will be like a garden in early spring, with plants springing up everywhere."

Nigeria shall know joy again

Prayer Point 4

- Pray for the joy of the Lord to spring up everywhere in Nigeria.
- Declare that every prophetic word over Nigeria shall be activated and we shall do our utmost to see them come to pass in our time.

10

WATCHMEN ROLE FULLY RESTORED

CHAPTER TEN
PRAYER DAY 10

WATCHMEN ROLE FULLY RESTORED

Prayer Quote

"The little estimate we put on prayer is evidence from the little time we give to it." E.M. Bounds

Daniel 6:10

"Now when Daniel knew that the writing was signed, he went into his house; and his windows being open in his chamber toward Jerusalem, he kneeled upon his knees three times a day, and prayed, and gave thanks before his God, as he did aforetime."

Blazing Righteousness

Isaiah 62:1-3 (MSG)

"Regarding Zion, I can't keep my mouth shut, regarding Jerusalem, I can't hold my tongue, until her righteousness blazes down like the sun and her salvation flames up like a torch.

Foreign countries will see your righteousness, and world leaders your glory. You'll get a brand-new name straight from the mouth of God.

You'll be a stunning crown in the palm of God's hand, a jeweled gold cup held high in the hand of your God."

Prayer Point 1

- Thank the Lord for His commitment to ensure that Nigeria will produce blazing righteousness and unprecedented salvation.

- Let's proclaim that people from far flung lands and those not in covenant with our God will see the glory of God upon us and be drawn to it.
- Declare that we will be called by our new prophetic names which the Lord Himself has given us and no longer will we be addressed by any unpleasant name.
- Pray that we will be held high by God as a stunning crown and a gold jewelled cup in God's Hand!

Your God Will Delight In You

Isaiah 62:4-5 (MSG)

"No more will anyone call you Rejected, and your country will no more be called Ruined. You'll be called Hephzibah (My Delight), and your land Beulah (Married), Because God delights in you and your land will be like a wedding celebration.

For as a young man marries his virgin bride, so your builder marries you, And as a bridegroom is happy in his bride, so your God is happy with you."

Prayer Point 2

- Come against every form of rejection and neglect we have suffered previously and declare that just like present day Israel, the Lord will delight in us and will RESTORE us to the prophetic place He has ordained for us.
- Let's prayerfully reclaim every LAND which means every spiritual, emotional and physical place presently still under darkness, to be as glorious as the Land the LORD has given to us for our inheritance as Nigerians.
- Declare we will have everything God has for us and command everything

that has been delayed and long overdue to manifest in our nation.

- Pray that we will be married to our prophetic promises as a young man marries his wife and we will not be separated from our God ordained place.
- Ask the LORD to DELIGHT IN NIGERIA as a bridegroom delights in his bride and that our ways will please the LORD.

Keeping God in Remembrance

Isaiah 62:6-7 (MSG)

"I've posted watchmen on your walls, Jerusalem. Day and night they keep at it, praying, calling out, and reminding God to remember.
They are to give him no peace until he does what he said, until he makes Jerusalem famous as the City of Praise."

Prayer Point 3

- Ask the Lord to continually remind you of your role as a set watchman upon the walls of Nigeria and that you will not fail in your prayer place.
- Ask the Lord to help you maintain a consistent and effective prayer life.
- Call forth the assigned churches and watchmen to get upon their city walls to SPEARHEAD prayer and raise God's ARK over the nation and continually PLEA for His intervention.
- Empower God's angels over these cities to work with the watchmen.
- Pray that these seven cities will be rallying points as watchmen come from the surrounding cities and from all over the world to join the spiritual warfare effort.
- Pray that the four winds of Judgement, Transformation, Restoration and

Righteousness blow across these cities till they reach every part of the nation.

- Proclaim that this prayer momentum will continue until Nigeria is called a house of prayer for all nations.
- Let's prophetically declare that great and glorious encounters will take place in our country, and a great move of God will break-forth in cities across Nigeria that will spread around the world.

Never Again

Isaiah 62:8-9 (MSG)

"God has taken a solemn oath, an oath he means to keep: "Never again will I open your grain-filled barns to your enemies to loot and eat. Never again will foreigners drink the wine that you worked so hard to produce.

No. The farmers who grow the food will eat the food and praise God for it. And those who make the wine will drink the wine in my holy courtyards."

Prayer Point 4

- Declare that never again will we sow and others reap, never again will those who oppose us take what is rightfully ours, never again will God allow our enemies have advantage over us.
- Proclaim that all our years of labour will finally be rewarded and we will be filled with praise to God for it.

Sought After

Isaiah 62:10-12 (MSG)

"Walk out of the gates. Get going! Get the road ready for the people. Build the highway. Get at it! Clear the debris, hoist high a flag, a signal to all peoples!

Yes! God has broadcast to all the world: "Tell daughter Zion, 'Look! Your Saviour comes, Ready to do what he said he'd do, prepared to complete what he promised.'

Zion will be called new names: Holy People, God-Redeemed, Sought-Out, City-Not-Forsaken."

Prayer Point 5

- Prayerfully remove every obstacle before us and make a highway for God's glory to come through to us and go to the ends of the earth.
- Declare that God's visitation upon us is sure and His MULTIPLE RESTORATION is irreversible and that He will fulfil all His promises over us.
- Declare all these prophetic names over us: Holy People, God Redeemed, Sought-Out, City Not Forsaken.

11

DAY OF VENGEANCE & YEAR OF REDEMPTION

CHAPTER ELEVEN
PRAYER DAY 11

DAY OF VENGEANCE & YEAR OF REDEMPTION

Prayer Quote

Colossians 4:12

"Epaphras, who is one of you, a servant of Christ, saluteth you, always labouring fervently for you in prayers that ye stand perfect and complete in all the will of God."

Announcing God's Judgment on the Wicked

Isaiah 63:1-6 (NLT)

"Who is this who comes from Edom, from the city of Bozrah, with his clothing stained red? Who is this in royal robes, marching in his great strength? "It is I, the Lord, announcing your salvation! It is I, the Lord, who has the power to save!"

Why are your clothes so red, as if you have been treading out grapes?

"I have been treading the winepress alone; no one was there to help me. In my anger I have trampled my enemies as if they were grapes.

In my fury I have trampled my foes.

Their blood has stained my clothes.

For the time has come for me to avenge my people, to ransom them from their oppressors.

I was amazed to see that no one intervened to help the oppressed. So I myself stepped in to save them with my strong arm, and my wrath sustained me.

I crushed the nations in my anger and made them stagger and fall to the ground, spilling their blood upon the earth."

The LORD will arise and judge the Wasters who have oppressed the Worried Ones for so long.
He will require the blood of the innocent that have been shed without justice at the hand of the oppressor.
It will be a time of unparralled divine judgment from the Lord.

Prayer Point 1

- Ask the Lord to arise and avenge the worried ones, the oppressed, the voiceless, the hopeless, and the helpless whose cry for help have fallen on deaf ears.
- That His judgment upon the wicked Wasters will be swift and carried out with divine finality.

Nigeria: God's Peculiar State (GPS)

Isaiah 63:7-14

"I will tell of the Lord's unfailing love. I will praise the Lord for all he has done. I will rejoice in his great goodness to Israel, which he has granted according to his mercy and love. He said, "They are my very own people. Surely they will not betray me again." And he became their Savior. In all their suffering he also suffered, and he personally rescued them. In his love and mercy he redeemed them. He lifted them up and carried them through all the years. But they rebelled against him and grieved his Holy Spirit. So he became their enemy and fought against them. Then they remembered those days of old when Moses led his people out of Egypt. They cried out, "Where is the one who brought Israel through the sea, with Moses as their shepherd? Where is the one who sent his Holy Spirit to be among his people? Where is the one whose power was displayed when Moses lifted up his hand—the one who divided the sea before them making himself famous forever? Where is the one who led them through the bottom of the sea? They were like fine stallions racing through the desert, never stumbling. As with cattle going down into a peaceful valley the Spirit of the Lord gave them rest You led your people, Lord, and gained a magnificent reputation."

Prayer Point 2

- Let's thank God for His unfailing love towards Nigeria and His peculiar love for us as a people. A prophetic GPS for other nations to follow our example in our service to God.
- Thank the LORD for His many mercies upon Nigeria and how He has preserved us till today through many trials yet we remain as one nation.
- Ask the Lord to make His name famous in Nigeria, through Nigeria and for Nigeria and that we will always remember that we are God's Peculiar State (GPS).

Prayer for Mercy and Pardon

Isaiah 63:15-19

"Lord, look down from heaven; look from your holy, glorious home, and see us. Where is the passion and the might you used to show on our behalf? Where are your mercy and compassion now? Surely you are still our Father! Even if Abraham and Jacob would disown us, Lord, you would still be our Father. You are our Redeemer from ages past. Lord, why have you allowed us to turn from your path? Why have you given us stubborn hearts so we no longer fear you? Return and help us, for we are your servants, the tribes that are your special possession. How briefly your holy people possessed your holy place, and now our enemies have destroyed it. Sometimes it seems as though we never belonged to you, as though we had never been known as your people."

The Lord still remains our first love in spite of our many short comings.

Prayer Point 3

- Remind the Lord of His compassion and ask Him to restore us to our first love.
- Ask for His forgiveness in any way that we have taken His grace for granted.
- Pray that He will return to us again in mercy and rid us of our stubbornness and many frailties.

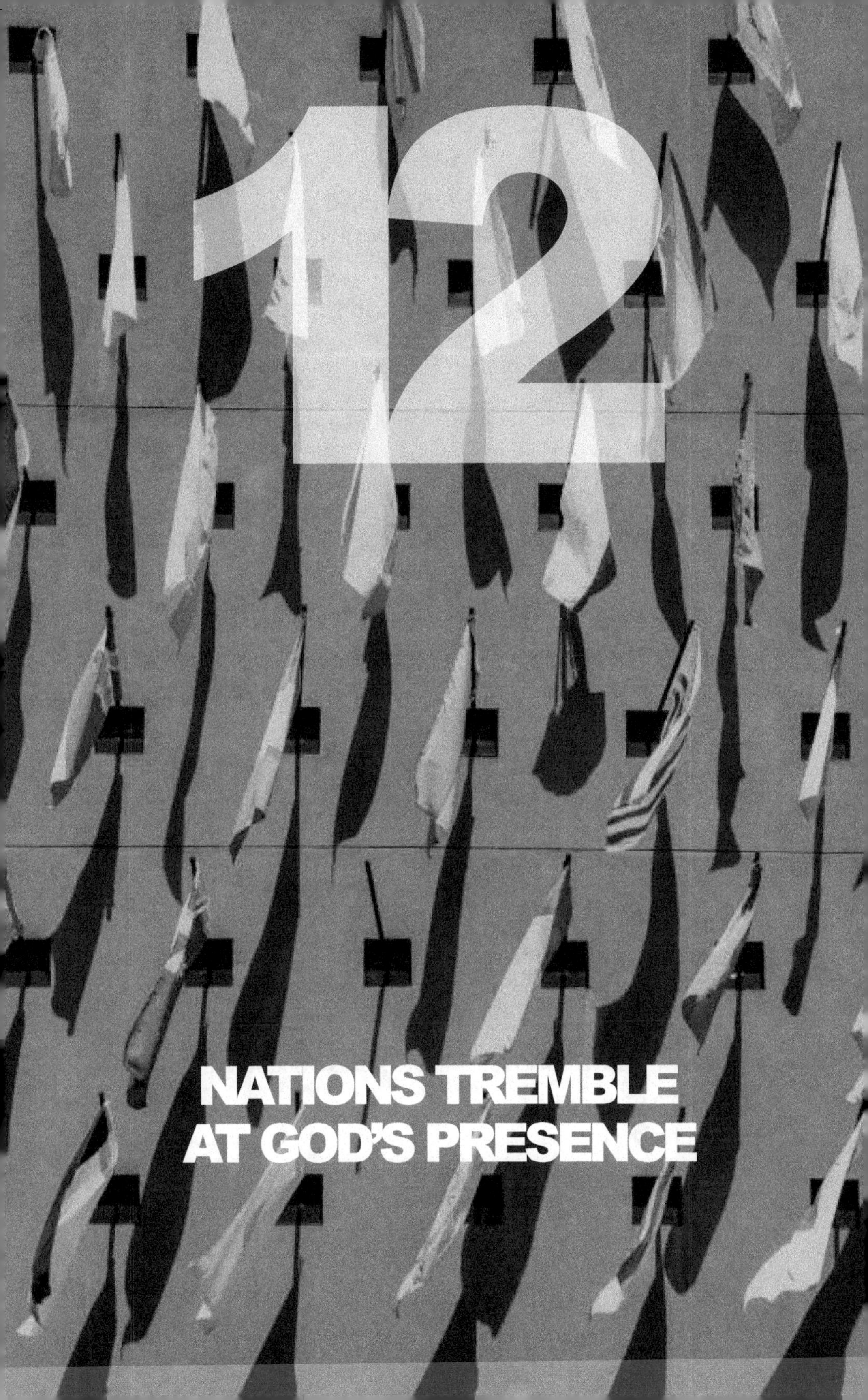

12

NATIONS TREMBLE AT GOD'S PRESENCE

CHAPTER TWELVE
PRAYER DAY 12

NATIONS TREMBLE AT GOD'S PRESENCE

Prayer Quote:

"No learning can make up for the failure to pray. No earnestness, no diligence, no study, no gifts will supply its lack." E.M. Bounds

Prayers for God's Unprecedented Presence

Isaiah 64:1-3 (NLT)

"Oh, that you would burst from the heavens and come down! How the mountains would quake in your presence! As fire causes wood to burn and water to boil, your coming would make the nations tremble. Then your enemies would learn the reason for your fame! When you came down long ago, you did awesome deeds beyond our highest expectations. And oh, how the mountains quaked!"

None can resist His Presence

Prayer Point 1

- Let every watchman desperately cry out for God's mountain melting presence.
- Command all the mountains (corruption, oppression, visionlessness, etc.) that have stood against Nigeria in all spheres of society to melt away like wax before the fire.
- Pray that the nations will marvel at the great things the Lord will do in Nigeria in these days and that He will exceed all our expectations.

No one like our God

Isaiah 64:4

"For since the world began, no ear has heard and no eye has seen a God like you, who works for those who wait for him!"

Our God does what no other can do

Prayer Point 2

- Praise the Lord for there is absolutely no God like Him.
- Thank Him because He always shows Himself strong on behalf of those who fear and love Him.

Repent some more

Isaiah 64:5-12

"You welcome those who gladly do good, who follow godly ways. But you have been very angry with us, for we are not godly. We are constant sinners; how can people like us be saved? We are all infected and impure with sin. When we display our righteous deeds, they are nothing but filthy rags. Like autumn leaves, we wither and fall, and our sins sweep us away like the wind. Yet no one calls on your name or pleads with you for mercy. Therefore, you have turned away from us and turned us over to our sins. And yet, O Lord, you are our Father. We are the clay, and you are the potter. We all are formed by your hand. Don't be so angry with us, Lord. Please don't remember our sins forever. Look at us, we pray, and see that we are all your people. Your holy cities are destroyed. Zion is a wilderness; yes, Jerusalem is a desolate ruin. The holy and beautiful Temple where our ancestors praised you has been burned down, and all the things of beauty are destroyed. After all this, Lord, must you still refuse to help us? Will you continue to be silent and punish us?"

God will never lower His standards, so it's up to us to step up to His standards of righteousness

Prayer Point 3

- Let's cry out some more for His unending mercy lest we be swept away by our sins and miss out on our personal prophecy as a nation.
- Ask for His mercy upon the watchmen that have either abandoned or fallen asleep on their watches. That all watchmen over Nigeria will arise from their slumber and earnestly seek His face.

13
FALSE PROPHETS &
ALTARS GIVE WAY TO
THE TRUE

CHAPTER THIRTEEN

PRAYER DAY 13

FALSE PROPHETS & ALTARS GIVE WAY TO THE TRUE

Prayer Quote

"Satan trembles when he sees the weakest Christian on his knees." William Cowper

Judgment and Final Salvation

Isaiah 65:1-7 (NLT)

"The Lord says, "I was ready to respond, but no one asked for help. I was ready to be found, but no one was looking for me. I said, 'Here I am, here I am!' to a nation that did not call on my name. All day long I opened my arms to a rebellious people. But they follow their own evil paths and their own crooked schemes. All day long they insult me to my face by worshiping idols in their sacred gardens. They burn incense on pagan altars. At night they go out among the graves, worshiping the dead. They eat the flesh of pigs and make stews with other forbidden foods. Yet they say to each other, 'Don't come too close or you will defile me! I am holier than you!' These people are a stench in my nostrils, an acrid smell that never goes away. "Look, my decree is written out in front of me: I will not stand silent; I will repay them in full! Yes, I will repay them—both for their own sins and for those of their ancestors," says the Lord. "For they also burned incense on the mountains and insulted me on the hills. I will pay them back in full!"

The Wasters in Nigeria depend heavily on false priests and false prophets to perpetuate the wicked deeds.

God shall visit them for their sins.

They shall be exposed by His mighty Hand and judged accordingly.

Prayer Point 1

- Ask the Lord to judge evil prophets and priests in the nation.
- That the Lord will cut off these false prophets and sorcerers and disconnect them from their altars like He did against the prophets of Baal in the time of Elijah.
- Pray that the Lord will raise men and women with a potent anointing like Elijah, Elisha and Jehu to cut off these false prophets and priests.

God always has a Remnant

Isaiah 65:8-9

“But I will not destroy them all,” says the Lord. “For just as good grapes are found among a cluster of bad ones (and someone will say, 'Don't throw them all away some of those grapes are good!'),so I will not destroy all Israel. For I still have true servants there. I will preserve a remnant of the people of Israel and of Judah to possess my land. Those I choose will inherit it, and my servants will live there."

God will show mercy to any sinner or backslider who genuinely repents and turns from his wicked ways

Prayer Point 2

- Pray for salvation of sinners and for the backslider to repent and return to the LORD.

Those who seek the Lord shall find Him

Isaiah 65:10

"The plain of Sharon will again be filled with flocks for my people who have searched for me, and the valley of Achor will be a place to pasture herds".

There has to be a hunger for righteousness before there can be an outpouring of blessings

Prayer Point 3

- Pray for a deep hunger in the hearts of Nigerians to return to the God of Abraham, Isaac and Jacob.
- Pray for abundance to every God seeker in the nation.

The idols of Nigeria shall be Judged

Isaiah 65:11-15

"But because the rest of you have forsaken the Lord and have forgotten his Temple, and because you have prepared feasts to honor the god of Fate and have offered mixed wine to the god of Destiny, now I will 'destine' you for the sword. All of you will bow down before the executioner. For when I called, you did not answer. When I spoke, you did not listen.

You deliberately sinned—before my very eyes and chose to do what you know I despise." Therefore, this is what the Sovereign Lord says: "My servants will eat, but you will starve. My servants will drink, but you will be thirsty. My servants will rejoice, but you will be sad and ashamed. My servants will sing for joy, but you will cry in sorrow and despair. Your name will be a curse word among my people, for the Sovereign Lord will destroy you and will call his true servants by another name."

There will be a distinction between those who serve God and those who are hypocrites

Prayer Point 4

- Pray that God's hand will be heavy against every hypocrite who is proclaiming to be worshipping God but in secret is worshipping idols.
- Judge all the idols of the hearts and declare there is clear difference between true prophets from false prophets.

Nigeria shall be a most desirable destination

Isaiah 65:16-25

"All who invoke a blessing or take an oath will do so by the God of truth. For I will put aside my anger and forget the evil of earlier days. "Look! I am creating new heavens and a new earth, and no one will even think about the old ones anymore. Be glad; rejoice forever in my creation! And look! I will create Jerusalem as a place of happiness. Her people will be a source of joy. I will rejoice over Jerusalem and delight in my people. And the sound of weeping and crying will be heard in it no more. "No longer will babies die when only a few days old. No longer will adults die before they have lived a full life. No longer will people be considered old at one hundred! Only the cursed will die that young! In those days people will live in the houses they build and eat the fruit of their own vineyards. Unlike the past, invaders will not take their houses and confiscate their vineyards. For my people will live as long as trees, and my chosen ones will have time to enjoy their hard-won gains. They will not work in vain, and their children will not be doomed to misfortune. For they are people blessed by the Lord, and their children, too, will be blessed. I will answer them before they even call to me. While they are still talking about their needs, I will go ahead and answer their prayers! The wolf and the lamb will feed together. The lion will eat hay like a cow. But the snakes will eat dust. In those days no one will be hurt or destroyed on my holy mountain. I, the Lord, have spoken!"

For the generation that can pay the price they shall see Nigeria become a most desirable nation

Prayer Point 5

- Pray that we are that generation that will deliver on the promise of the Nigeria of our dreams.
- That in this new country, what was a far-fetched and even an unthinkable possibility will become our daily reality. That peace, security and great prosperity will be our new normal.

14

A NEW NATION IS
BORN AT ONCE

CHAPTER FOURTEEN
PRAYER DAY 14

A NEW NATION IS BORN AT ONCE

Prayer Quote

"Prayer will make a man cease from sin, or sin will entice a man to cease from prayer." John Bunyon

Yes to a New Nation

Isaiah 66:1-2 (NLT)

"This is what the Lord says: "Heaven is my throne, and the earth is my footstool. Could you build me a temple as good as that? Could you build me such a resting place? My hands have made both heaven and earth; they and everything in them are mine. I, the Lord, have spoken! "I will bless those who have humble and contrite hearts, who tremble at my word."

God gives grace to the humble in spirit

Prayer Point 1

- Pray that the company of God fearers-the Watchmen, the Warriors and Wise Ones will increase greatly.
- That we will humble ourselves at the feet of JESUS CHRIST and keep company with those who tremble at His word.

God Rejects Lip Service

Isaiah 66:3-4

"But those who choose their own ways delighting in their detestable sins will not have their offerings accepted. When such people sacrifice a bull, it is no more acceptable than a human sacrifice. When they sacrifice a lamb, it's as though they had sacrificed a dog! When they bring an offering of grain, they might as well offer the blood of a pig. When they burn frankincense, it's as if they had blessed an idol. I will send them great trouble all the things they feared. For when I called, they did not answer. When I spoke, they did not listen.They deliberately sinned before my very eyes and chose to do what they know I despise."

God will reject insincere sacrifices and will no more put up with religion

Prayer Point 2

- Pray against the spirit of the Pharisees and Sadducees who worship God only with their lips but their hearts are far from God.

When Zion travails

Isaiah 66:5-9

"Hear this message from the Lord, all you who tremble at his words: "Your own people hate you and throw you out for being loyal to my name. 'Let the Lord be honored!' they scoff. 'Be joyful in him!'But they will be put to shame. What is all the commotion in the city? What is that terrible noise from the Temple? It is the voice of the Lord taking vengeance against his enemies. "Before the birth pains even begin, Jerusalem gives birth to a son.

Who has ever seen anything as strange as this? Who ever heard of such a thing? Has a nation ever been born in a single day? Has a country ever come forth in a mere moment? But by the time Jerusalem's birth pains begin, her children will be born. Would I ever bring this nation to the point of birth and then not deliver it?" asks the Lord. "No! I would never keep this nation from being born," says your God."

God is going to stand up for the persecuted who have been mocked for standing up for godliness.
The revival of Nigeria will reach its peak as a new country comes forth.

Prayer Point 3

- Pray for the voice of God's true prophets to become the most significant and most respected voice in the nation. Silence every contrary voice.
- Pray that God's watchmen will travail intensely until a New Nation finally emerges from the womb of prayer.
- Pray that this miracle will be similar to the birthing of Israel when Moses and his people emerged from the Red Sea. That many will be astonished by this incredible miracle.

Rejoice in the New Nation

Isaiah 66:10-14

"Rejoice with Jerusalem! Be glad with her, all you who love her and all you who mourn for her. Drink deeply of her glory even as an infant drinks at its mother's comforting breasts." This is what the Lord says: "I will give Jerusalem a river of peace and prosperity. The wealth of the nations will flow to her. Her children will be nursed at her breasts, carried in her arms, and held on her lap. I will comfort you there in Jerusalem as a mother comforts her child." When you see these things, your heart will rejoice. You will flourish like the grass! Everyone will see the Lord's hand of blessing on his servants and his anger against his enemies."

It will be time of jubilation in Nigeria

Prayer Point 4

- Pray that Nigeria will enter into her year of spiritual Jubilee and her citizens shall deeply take delight in her prosperity.

Nigeria as a Revival Centre

Isaiah 66:15-24

"See, the Lord is coming with fire, and his swift chariots roar like a whirlwind. He will bring punishment with the fury of his anger and the flaming fire of his hot rebuke. The Lord will punish the world by fire and by his sword. He will judge the earth, and many will be killed by him. "Those who 'consecrate' and 'purify' themselves in a sacred garden with its idol in the center—feasting on pork and rats and other detestable meats—will come to a terrible end," says the Lord. "I can see what they are doing, and I know what they are thinking. So I will gather all nations and peoples together, and they will see my glory. I will perform a sign among them. And I will send those who survive to be messengers to the nations—to Tarshish, to the Libyans and Lydians (who are famous as archers), to Tubal and Greece, and to all the lands beyond the sea that have not heard of my fame or seen my glory.

There they will declare my glory to the nations. They will bring the remnant of your people back from every nation. They will bring them to my holy mountain in Jerusalem as an offering to the Lord. They will ride on horses, in chariots and wagons, and on mules and camels," says the Lord. "And I will appoint some of them to be my priests and Levites. I, the Lord, have spoken!"

"As surely as my new heavens and earth will remain, so will you always be my people, with a name that will never disappear," says the Lord. "All humanity will come to worship me from week to week and from month to month.And as they go out, they will see the dead bodies of those who have rebelled against me. For the worms that devour them will never die, and the fire that burns them will never go out. All who pass by will view them with utter horror."

Nigeria shall begin to manifest her full prophetic mantle and mandate.

Prayer Point 5

- Pray that Nigeria will be one of the most prominent end times revival centres and remain a frontline missionary sending nation.
- Pray that many more Nigerians in the Diaspora shall return to join this incredible harvest.

WEEK THREE

THIRD PROPHECY ON SYMBOLS OF HIS GLORY (RECEIVED 2018)

BACKGROUND: THE SYMBOLS OF HIS GLORY

1 Samuel 1: 2-3 NLT
"There was a man named Elkanah who lived in Ramah in the region of Zuph in the hill country of Ephraim. He was the son of Jeroham, son of Elihu, son of Tohu, son of Zuph, of Ephraim. Elkanah had two wives, Hannah and Peninnah. Peninnah had children, but Hannah did not."

Elkanah had two Wives

Penninah was very fruitful but Hannah had no fruit of the womb to show she was a married woman.

Hannah may ordinarily have settled for barrenness if she was the only wife but her rival would not let her.

Although Hannah got a double portion she still couldn't get more than the combined portions of her rival and her children.

Penninah made Hannah's life a living hell. She taunted and mocked Hannah in the area of her deficiency

Penninah sustained this persecution year after year until Hannah was reduced to tears every time and would not even eat the double portion her husband gave her.

We have a relentless enemy that will not let us be until we cannot enjoy even the little that we have.

These taunting and relentless attacks didn't stop until Hannah took action.

The enemy will never call for a ceasefire, he doesn't understand compassion or mercy, he only knows how to steal, kill & destroy.

John 10:10
"The thief cometh not, but for to steal, and to kill, and to destroy: I am come that they might have life, and that they might have it more abundantly."

One woman's prayer made JUST ONCE changed the destiny of a nation.

Vs 9: "Once after a sacrificial meal at Shiloh, Hannah got up and went to pray"

Severely persecuted by her rival.
Misunderstood by her beloved husband.

Vs 8: "Why are you crying, Hannah?" Elkanah would ask. "Why aren't you eating? Why be downhearted just because you have no children? You have me—isn't that better than having ten sons?"

Misunderstood by her pastor (High Priest Eli), who alleged she was drunk in church.
She made a vow to the only one that knew where this was headed.
God used her pain, her weakness and her barrenness to ignite an incredible power of prayer in Hannah that made heaven answer with a resounding "Yes".
While Peninnah had so many children, they achieved so little that their

names were not worthy of mention in the Bible.
However Hannah's first son born out of pain was such a remarkable man that two books of the Bible were named after him.
Hannah further had three more sons and two daughters ...that's six children in all.

The seven different aspects of Hannah's heartfelt vow and prayers:

- She was very private about it...she only told her husband later.
- She was very sincere about her pain, she poured her soul out to the Lord, she said it as she felt it.
- She was very specific about wanting a son, if a daughter came instead then she could consider it not a fulfilment of the vow but just God's providence.
- She was very clear that she would give him to God as a Nazarene for all his life.

This was a hard one, how could this woman who wanted a child so badly promise to give him up to God?. At least maybe she could have asked for two sons and then given one for God's service.
I thank God for praying mothers who sort out their children and family in prayers.
I got radically saved and thought it was just between me and God until one day my cousin who knew the full story told me how my mum always asked him to pray with her in agreement that I get saved and serve God completely.
Guess what? She is now in heaven but the fruit of her prayers still lives on...I am still serving the God she dedicated me to just as Hannah did for Samuel and I am loving it every day.

- She made only one vow all her life and kept it.

Vows are not to be made before God carelessly. Hannah only made one vow in her life and kept it.

- She got a word on the matter.

Vs 17 "In that case," Eli said, "Go in peace! May the God of Israel grant the request you have asked of him."

Make sure when you are seeking God on a serious matter that you get a Rhema on the issue.

Prayer is NEVER A MONOLOGUE BUT A DIALOGUE with GOD.

If you haven't heard from Him loud and clear, keep praying and keep waiting.

- She was no longer sad after she had received the comforting word from the High Priest.

Why should you still be worried after an effective prayer like that? It's a sign you are not walking in faith.

The Bigger Picture

While what we see initially in our text is the rivalry between Penninah and Hannah the truth is that there was something much bigger.

God actually was tired of the Priesthood of Eli and his sinful sons....and was seeking an alternative.

The problem of any society where the true Church exists can be traced to the failure of the light and salt to do what God designed for it to do.

Too many times we point at symptoms and say "it's the political class", "it's the economic situation", "it's this", "it's that"....While these classes or causes cannot be exonerated, they are only signs of an existing root cause.

Eli's sons were desecrating God's Temple and Eli failed to bring them under effective discipline.

1 Samuel 2:12-18 NLT

“Now the sons of Eli were scoundrels who had no respect for the Lord or for their duties as priests. Whenever anyone offered a sacrifice, Eli's sons would send over a servant with a three-pronged fork. While the meat of the sacrificed animal was still boiling, The servant would stick the fork into the pot and demand that whatever it brought up be given to Eli's sons. All the Israelites who came to worship at Shiloh were treated this way. Sometimes the servant would come even before the animal's fat had been burned on the altar. He would demand raw meat before it had been boiled so that it could be used for roasting. The man offering the sacrifice might reply, “Take as much as you want, but the fat must be burned first.” Then the servant would demand, “No, give it to me now, or I'll take it by force.” So the sin of these young men was very serious in the Lord's sight, for they treated the Lord's offerings with contempt. But Samuel, though he was only a boy, served the Lord. He wore a linen garment like that of a priest.”

1 Samuel 2:22-26 NLT

"Now Eli was very old, but he was aware of what his sons were doing to the people of Israel. He knew, for instance, that his sons were seducing the young women who assisted at the entrance of the Tabernacle. Eli said to them, “I have been hearing reports from all the people about the wicked things you are doing. Why do you keep sinning? You must stop, my sons! The reports I hear among the Lord's people are not good. If someone sins against another person, God can mediate for the guilty party. But if someone sins against the Lord, who can intercede?” But Eli's sons wouldn't listen to their father, for the Lord was already planning to put them to death. Meanwhile, the boy Samuel grew taller and grew in favor with the Lord and with the people."

God sent a prophet to announce His intentions to judge Eli & his sons.

1 Samuel 2:27-36 NLT
"One day a man of God came to Eli and gave him this message from the Lord: "I revealed myself to your ancestors when they were Pharaoh's slaves in Egypt. I chose your ancestor Aaron from among all the tribes of Israel to be my priest, to offer sacrifices on my altar, to burn incense, and to wear the priestly vest as he served me. And I assigned the sacrificial offerings to you priests. So why do you scorn my sacrifices and offerings? Why do you give your sons more honor than you give me—for you and they have become fat from the best offerings of my people Israel! "Therefore, the Lord, the God of Israel, says: I promised that your branch of the tribe of Levi would always be my priests. But I will honor those who honor me, and I will despise those who think lightly of me. The time is coming when I will put an end to your family, so it will no longer serve as my priests. All the members of your family will die before their time. None will reach old age. You will watch with envy as I pour out prosperity on the people of Israel. But no members of your family will ever live out their days. The few not cut off from serving at my altar will survive, but only so their eyes can go blind and their hearts break, and their children will die a violent death. And to prove that what I have said will come true, I will cause your two sons, Hophni and Phinehas, to die on the same day! "Then I will raise up a faithful priest who will serve me and do what I desire. I will establish his family, and they will be priests to my

anointed kings forever. Then all of your surviving family will bow before him, begging for money and food. 'Please,' they will say, 'give us jobs among the priests so we will have enough to eat.'"

PROPHECY: NIGERIA HAS TWO WIVES just like Elkanah

Penninah has more children and she is persecuting Hannah severely.
Out of this pain Hannah has given birth to a new prophetic order. A Samuel Company.
The problem with the nation and the persecution of Hannah by Penninah will not stop until Hannah pours her soul out to the Lord and her son is weaned.
The bigger picture is that God is changing the priestly order. He will remove Eli and his sons who have become dull of hearing.

1 Samuel 3:1 NLT
"Meanwhile, the boy Samuel served the Lord by assisting Eli. Now in those days messages from the Lord were very rare, and visions were quite uncommon."

Hophni and Phinehas are desecrating the Temple and sleeping around...making it a den of thieves instead of the House of Prayer for all Nations.
Eli's entire Priesthood has lost respect and honor in the Land and his children refuse to obey him.
As a result there is no fear of God in the land...it's all a show. There is no clear distinction between the true and false prophets in the Land.
When Philip entered Samaria, Simon the Sorcerer's deception was shut

down instantly, he couldn't operate in the land anymore

But when you see a sorcerer being mistaken for a true prophet then you know Eli and his sons are at the verge of divine judgment.

The Fate of Nigeria is Similar to the First 7 Chapters of the Book 1 Samuel

Chapter 1. Penninah and Hannah.

Birth of Samuel and his dedication to God.

A new Priesthood (Samuel generation) will emerge out of great persecution and pain of Hannah.

Chapter 2. God Raising Samuel to replace Eli's Priesthood

The sins of the sons of Eli has resulted in divine revocation of the personal prophecies over their priesthood

God is sending several prophetic warnings to Eli.

The old Priesthood has failed.

Chapter 3. The Word of God is scarce but God starts speaking to Samuel

Samuel confirmed as God's new official channel...bigger and better.

God will fine tune His call upon His new priesthood who will differ from Eli's priesthood as this one will carry a 3-fold anointing of Prophet, Priest & Judge and seal the judgment determined against the failed priesthood.

This Samuel order has the 3-fold anointing of Watchman, Warrior and Wise One.

Chapter 4. Symbols of God's glory taken away.

Judgment of the old priesthood (three generations of Eli will be judged: Eli,

Hophni & Phinehas and Ichabod)

Phinehas' son is named Ichabod (where is the glory) by His dying mother. What ever happened to Ichabod? He is only mentioned one more time **(1 Samuel14:3)** in passing and never did amount to much.

Chapter 5 & 6. God defends His glory among the Philistines.

God fights for His glory. The Ark is returned by the Philistines to Israel.

Chapter 7. National Repentance. New Prophetic Order.

Samuel calls for a national day of repentance as the nation turns back to God.

15

THE GATHERING AT MIZPAH

CHAPTER FIFTEEN
PRAYER DAY 15

THE GATHERING AT MIZPAH

Prayer Quote

"He who has learned to pray has learned the greatest secret of a holy and happy life." William Law.

Symbols of God's glory cannot replace him

1 Samuel 4:1-22 NLT

"And Samuel's words went out to all the people of Israel. The Philistines Capture the Ark. At that time Israel was at war with the Philistines. The Israelite army was camped near Ebenezer, and the Philistines were at Aphek. The Philistines attacked and defeated the army of Israel, killing 4,000 men. After the battle was over, the troops retreated to their camp, and the elders of Israel asked, "Why did the Lord allow us to be defeated by the Philistines?" Then they said, "Let's bring the Ark of the Covenant of the Lord from Shiloh. If we carry it into battle with us, it will save us from our enemies." So they sent men to Shiloh to bring the Ark of the Covenant of the Lord of Heaven's Armies, who is enthroned between the cherubim. Hophni and Phinehas, the sons of Eli, were also there with the Ark of the Covenant of God. When all the Israelites saw the Ark of the Covenant of the Lord coming into the camp, their shout of joy was so loud it made the ground shake!

"What's going on?" the Philistines asked. "What's all the shouting about in the Hebrew camp?" When they were told it was because the Ark of the Lord had arrived, they panicked. "The gods have come into their camp!" they cried."This is a disaster! We have never had to face anything like this before! Help! Who can save us from these mighty gods of Israel? They are the same gods who destroyed the Egyptians with plagues when Israel was in the wilderness. Fight as never before, Philistines! If you don't, we will become the Hebrews' slaves just as they have been ours! Stand up like men and fight!"So the Philistines fought desperately, and Israel was defeated again. The slaughter was great; 30,000 Israelite soldiers died that day. The survivors turned and fled to their tents.The Ark of God was captured, and Hophni and Phinehas, the two sons of Eli, were killed. A man from the tribe of Benjamin ran from the battlefield and arrived at Shiloh later that same day. He had torn his clothes and put dust on his head to show his grief. Eli was waiting beside the road to hear the news of the battle, for his heart trembled for the safety of the Ark of God. When the messenger arrived and told what had happened, an outcry resounded throughout the town. "What is all the noise about?" Eli asked. The messenger rushed over to Eli, who was ninety-eight years old and blind. He said to Eli, "I have just come from the battlefield—I was there this very day." "What happened, my son?" Eli demanded. "Israel has been defeated by the Philistines," the messenger replied. "The people have been slaughtered, and your two sons, Hophni and Phinehas, were also killed. And the Ark of God has been captured." When the messenger mentioned what had happened to the Ark of God, Eli fell backward from his seat beside the gate. He broke his neck and died, for he was old and overweight. He had been Israel's judge for forty years. Eli's daughter-in-law, the wife of Phinehas, was pregnant and near her time of delivery. When she heard that the Ark of God had been captured and that her father-in-law and husband were dead, she went into labor and gave birth. She died in childbirth, but before she passed away the midwives tried to encourage her. "Don't be afraid," they said. "You have a baby boy!" But she did not answer or pay attention to them. She named the child Ichabod (which means "Where is the glory?"), for she said, "Israel's glory is gone." She named him this because the Ark of God had been captured and because her father-in-law and husband were dead."

The children of Israel went to war with the Philistines and lost 4,000 men in the first battle. They quickly sent for the Ark thinking they could use the "Symbol" of God's glory to their advantage while their priests where walking in utter disregard to God's law.

Well, in the second battle they were utterly humiliated as they lost 30,000 troops and the "Symbol" of God's presence was also captured for the first and last time in Israel's history.

This is what happens when God's people replace God's presence with "symbols", when we worship with no presence, when we pray with no presence and when we meet in His name but He is not there. Samson the Great was there too and it cost him his eyes, his dignity and brought his life to a premature end. The church has to take responsibility and get her acts together or else bloodshed will consume the nation in a short while those who are at ease in Zion will get a shock that will shake off their false sense of safety caused by the evil twins of complacency and compromise.

Prayer Point 1

- Let's pray earnestly that we will avert the calamity suffered by Israelites and their priesthood who were severely judged because they held on to the symbols rather than the presence and glory of God.
- Pray that God will spare His remnant as He brings about a sweeping change in the priesthood in our nation.

It's time to break up the fallow ground

Hosea 10:12

"Sow to yourselves in righteousness, reap in mercy; break up your fallow ground: for it is time to seek the LORD, till he come and rain righteousness upon you."

Just like Samuel we need to keep crying out to God for mercy

Prayer Point 2

- Let's break up every fallow ground of religion that has made our hearts so cold and insensitive to God's voice.
- Repent for what has made us to be more attracted to God's glory symbols rather than His person and presence.
- Let's repent on behalf of the priesthood for the abominable sins of Hophni and Phinehas.
- Pray that fathers of faith will effectively and quickly bring their unruly children to order before God's judgment overtakes them.

The Gathering at Mizpah: National Day of Repentance

1 Sam 7:1-14

"So the men of Kiriath-jearim came to get the Ark of the Lord. They took it to the hillside home of Abinadab and ordained Eleazar, his son, to be in charge of it. The Ark remained in Kiriath-jearim for a long time—twenty years in all. During that time all Israel mourned because it seemed the Lord had abandoned them.Then Samuel said to all the people of Israel, "If you want to return to the Lord with all your hearts, get rid of your foreign gods and your images of Ashtoreth. Turn your hearts to the Lord and obey him alone; then he will rescue you from the Philistines." So the Israelites got rid of their images of Baal and Ashtoreth and worshiped only the Lord. Then Samuel told them, "Gather all of Israel to Mizpah, and I will pray to the Lord for you." So they gathered at Mizpah and, in a great ceremony, drew water from a well and poured it out before the Lord. They also went without food all day and confessed that they had sinned against the Lord. (It was at Mizpah that Samuel became Israel's judge.) When the Philistine rulers heard that Israel had gathered at Mizpah, they mobilized their army and advanced. The Israelites were badly frightened when they learned that the Philistines were approaching. "Don't stop pleading with the Lord our God to save us from the Philistines!" they begged Samuel. So Samuel took a young lamb and offered it to the Lord as a whole burnt offering. He pleaded with the Lord to help Israel, and the Lord answered him. Just as Samuel was sacrificing the burnt offering, the Philistines arrived to attack Israel. But the Lord spoke with a mighty voice of thunder from heaven that day, and the Philistines were thrown into such confusion that the Israelites defeated them. The men of Israel chased them from Mizpah to a place below Beth-car, slaughtering them all along the way. Samuel then took a large stone and placed it between the towns of Mizpah and Jeshanah. He named it Ebenezer (which means "the stone of help"), for he said, "Up to this point the Lord has helped us!" So the Philistines were subdued and didn't invade Israel again for some time. And throughout Samuel's lifetime, the Lord's powerful hand was raised against the Philistines. The Israelite villages near Ekron and Gath that the Philistines had captured were restored to Israel, along with the rest of the territory that the Philistines had taken. And there was peace between Israel and the Amorites in those days."

Samuel the new prophet on the block called for a National Day of Repentance. The Israelites promptly obeyed and gathered at 'Mizpah' and put away all their idols and committed to serve God only.

Mizpah (Mizpeh) is Hebrew word meaning “May the Lord watch between us”, “watchtower” or “outlook post” (Genesis 31:44–49).

The Philistines got wind of it and assembled to attack, but the Israelites had learnt their lesson so they didn't go to fetch the Ark (symbol) but asked Samuel to keep crying (praying) to God for them.

Samuel prays and God sends thunder against the philistines and they suffer heavy losses and are thrown into commotion.

The men of Israel then attacked and the nation scored a major victory.

The Philistines never attacked Israel again all the days of Samuel's time as judge before he anointed King Saul and all the land previously taken by the Philistines were restored.

The Amorites (aspiring enemies) then made a peace treaty with Israel.

Prayer Point 3

- Pray that God's new prophetic order will call for NATIONAL DAY OF REPENTANCE and GATHERING AT MIZPAH.
- Pray that it will be a time of true repentance, when we will return to God of Abraham with all our hearts, put away all strange gods, prepare our hearts and serve Him only.

16

BACK TO THE BEGINNING - THE FEAR OF GOD

CHAPTER SIXTEEN
PRAYER DAY 16

BACK TO THE BEGINNING -THE FEAR OF GOD

Prayer Quote

"There is not in the world a kind of life more sweet and delightful than that of a continual conversation with God." Brother Lawrence

God Fearing Leadership

Hosea 3:5

"Afterward shall the children of Israel return, and seek the Lord their God, and David their king; and shall fear the LORD and his goodness in the latter days."

2 Samuel 23:3-4

"The God of Israel said, the Rock of Israel spake to me, He that ruleth over men MUST be just, ruling in the FEAR of God. And he shall be as the light of the morning, when the sun riseth, even a morning without clouds; as the tender grass springing out of the earth by clear shining after rain."

The scripture above speaks prophetically of a generation that will return to the fear of God, that generation will demand and produce a God-fearing leadership like King David - a God-loving and fearing man.

One of the key challenges we face as a people is that we do not really fear and reverence the Lord.

Nowhere is this disregard for the fear of God more evident than in leadership.

Leadership in Nigeria and indeed Africa goes unchecked, there is no fear of God at the heart of it all.

Prayer Point 1

- Let's prayerfully demand for a return of the fear of God at all levels of leadership.
- Pray for just and equitable leadership led in the fear of God.

God Fearing People

Deuteronomy 5:29

"O that there were such an heart in them, that they would fear me, and keep all my commandments always, that it might be well with them, and with their children for ever!"

Wow, the above text blew me away the first time I came across it (and it still does). Can you imagine for once that God actually has His own 'prayer request'? Enough of bombarding heaven with ONLY our request maybe it's time we pause and ask. LORD IS THERE ANY ONE THING YOU WILL HAVE ME DO FOR YOU FOR A CHANGE?

Friends I anticipate that His answer will not be far from: 'OH THAT THERE WHERE SUCH A HEART IN YOU TO FEAR ME ALWAYS'.

Prayer Point 2

- Oh pray that we as a people will respond to this STRONG DESIRE of God revealed here in **(Deuteronomy 5).**

- That you and I will hearken to God's heart cry for a God fearing generation.
- That He will give you SUCH A HEART as He expressly desires!

The Blessings upon the God fearers

2 Kings 17:38-39

"And the covenant that I have made with you ye shall not forget; neither shall ye fear other gods. But the Lord your God ye shall fear; and he shall deliver you out of the hand of all your enemies."

The blessing upon those that fear God include:

Free from fear of other gods.

Deliverance from all enemies no matter how many or how strong.

Unshakable confidence in battle.

Psalms 27:1-3

"The Lord is my light and my salvation; whom shall I fear? The LORD is the strength of my life; of whom shall I be afraid? When the wicked, even mine enemies and my foes, came upon me to eat up my flesh, they stumbled and fell. Though an host should encamp against me, my heart shall not fear: though war should rise against me, in this will I be confident."

Divine wisdom

Divine understanding

Job 28:28

"And unto man he said, Behold, the fear of the Lord, that is wisdom; and to depart from evil is understanding."

Purity that endures forever

Ps 19:9

"The fear of the LORD is clean, enduring for ever..."

The secrets of God are kept with God fearers.
The covenant of God. Covenant of everlasting faithfulness and friendship.

Psalms 25:14

"The secret of the Lord is with them that fear him; and he will shew them his covenant."

Long life
Well being
Mighty increase

Deuteronomy 6:2-3

"That thou mightest fear the Lord thy God, to keep all his statutes and his commandments, which I command thee, thou, and thy son, and thy son's son, all the days of thy life; and that thy days may be prolonged.Hear therefore, O Israel, and observe to do it; that it may be well with thee, and that ye may increase mightily, as the Lord God of thy fathers hath promised thee, in the land that floweth with milk and honey."

Prayer Point 3

- Now pronounce all the above blessings upon all those who will walk in fear of God including YOU (if you will fear Him).

The woes that will be upon those who don't fear the Lord

Proverbs 1:29-33

"For that they hated knowledge, and did not choose the fear of the Lord:

They would none of my counsel: they despised all my reproof. Therefore shall they eat of the fruit of their own way, and be filled with their own devices. For the turning away of the simple shall slay them, and the prosperity of fools shall destroy them. But whoso hearkeneth unto me shall dwell safely, and shall be quiet from fear of evil."

Psalms 36:1-4, 12

"The transgression of the wicked saith within my heart, that there is no fear of God before his eyes. For he flattereth himself in his own eyes, until his iniquity be found to be hateful. The words of his mouth are iniquity and deceit: he hath left off to be wise, and to do good. He deviseth mischief upon his bed; he setteth himself in a way that is not good; he abhorreth not evil. There are the workers of iniquity fallen: they are cast down, and shall not be able to rise."

For the wasters who refuse to turn from their wicked ways, well the Lord has an answer for them. they shall reap the fruits of their evil deeds, be filled with selfishness and be destroyed

They shall walk in self-deceit & pride, self-flattery until they are judged.

Depravation of wisdom, have no capacity to do good.

Inventors of mischief, love evil and hate good.

These Wasters will eventually fall and will not be able to rise.

Prayer Point 4

- Now raise strong intercessions and pronounce judgment upon the Wasters and all those who refuse to walk in the fear the LORD.
- That our leaders, political, religious etc will return to the fear of God or be

judged as stated in the scriptures above.

- That the citizenry will have ZERO tolerance for those who despise the fear of the Lord.
- That as a nation we must all go back to the beginning!

Proverbs 1:7

"The fear of the Lord is the beginning of knowledge: but fools despise wisdom and instruction."

17

TIME TO CONVERGE, CONNECT, CONVERSE AND TAKE COLLECTIVE ACTION

CHAPTER SEVENTEEN
PRAYER DAY 17

TIME TO CONVERGE, CONNECT, CONVERSE AND TAKE COLLECTIVE ACTION

Prayer Quote

When asked how much time he spent in prayer, George Muller's reply was, "Hours every day. But I live in the spirit of prayer. I pray as I walk and when I lie down and when I arise. And the answers are always coming." Anonymous.

Let the Princes of Africa CONVERGE

Psalms 68:31

"Princes shall come out of Egypt; Ethiopia shall soon stretch out her hands unto God."

Psalm 105:16-22

"He called for a famine on the land of Canaan, cutting off its food supply. Then he sent someone to Egypt ahead of them - Joseph, who was sold as a slave.They bruised his feet with fetters and placed his neck in an iron collar. Until the time came to fulfil his dreams, the Lord tested Joseph's character. Then Pharaoh sent for him and set him free; the ruler of the nation opened his prison door. Joseph was put in charge of all the king's household; he became ruler over all the king's possessions. He could instruct the king's aides as he pleased and teach the king's advisers."

God spoke to me some time ago about the plight of Africa and gave me a strong prophetic insight on the similarity of the experience of the Israelites in Egypt and that of Africans today.

Joseph was sold into slavery through the betrayal of his brothers.

The first set of Africans to migrate overseas were betrayed by their brothers who were enticed by the slave traders to betray their rival clans for monetary gain.

Joseph's gift helped to greatly empower Pharaoh and Egypt. Many Africans and indeed Nigerians in the diaspora are empowering other nations while their countries are under-developed.

Joseph's brothers and father later migrated to Egypt in search of bread.

The second set of Africans to migrate went in search of bread, in search of a better life.

When it was about time for their deliverance from slavery, God raised Moses in the palace of Pharaoh and as a prince in Egypt. He went through 40 years of obscurity in the wilderness

God has been preparing a Moses company in the background and in the most unlikely places.

After a long while God stirred Moses through a vision and sent him back to deliver His people from the clutches of Pharaoh.

It is God and not man that is stirring our hearts to do something for our nation and continent at this time.

That's why you have this book in your hand, that's why your heart has been bleeding for our nation because God is behind it all.

Prayer Point 1

- Pray that at this time princes will rise out of Africa.
- That you and I will be part of that prophetic company of REFORMERS (Warriors) and Watchmen and Wise ones.

Let Nigerians in Diaspora and Nigerians at home CONNECT

Exodus 4:27-31

"Now the Lord had said to Aaron, "Go out into the wilderness to meet Moses." So Aaron went and met Moses at the mountain of God, and he embraced him. Moses then told Aaron everything the Lord had commanded him to say. And he told him about the miraculous signs the Lord had commanded him to perform. Then Moses and Aaron returned to Egypt and called all the elders of Israel together. Aaron told them everything the Lord had told Moses, and Moses performed the miraculous signs as they watched. Then the people of Israel were convinced that the Lord had sent Moses and Aaron. When they heard that the Lord was concerned about them and had seen their misery, they bowed down and worshiped."

Moses HAD TO CONNECT and partner with his fellow Israelites in Egypt before their deliverance could be executed.

There has to be a global connection between Nigerians in Nigeria and Nigerians in the diaspora.

God has started stirring the hearts of a Moses company to do something about the plight of their people.

Prayer Point 2

- Ask the Lord to stir the heart of every Moses Company (REFORMERS in the diaspora) and Aaron Company (REFORMERS in Nigeria) to start CONNECTING and forge a way forward for our nation.

Let the CONVERSATION begin

2 Kings 7:3-7

"And there were four leprous men at the entering in of the gate: and they said one to another, why sit we here until we die? If we say, we will enter into the city, then the famine is in the city, and we shall die there: and if we sit still here, we die also. Now therefore come, and let us fall unto the host of the Syrians: if they save us alive, we shall live; and if they kill us, we shall but die. And they rose up in the twilight, to go unto the camp of the Syrians: and when they were come to the uttermost part of the camp of Syria, behold, there was no man there. For the Lord had made the host of the Syrians to hear a noise of chariots, and a noise of horses, even the noise of a great host: and they said one to another, lo, the king of Israel hath hired against us the kings of the Hittites, and the kings of the Egyptians, to come upon us. Wherefore they arose and fled in the twilight, and left their tents, and their horses, and their asses, even the camp as it was, and fled for their life."

The bible talks about the four lepers that sat at the gates of Samaria.

They suddenly began a CONVERSATION that brought about a mighty deliverance for the nation of Israel.

It is clear that the Lord waited for the lepers to move before He did, He was literally waiting for their cue.

Fearful as it may sound, God is in partnership with us and after He stirs our hearts He will wait for our cue.

Prayer Point 3

- Pray that we will stop looking at our limitations (leprosy) and start a CONVERSATION that will MOVE us forward as a nation.
- Pray that we will not sit around until we all die off without a change in our dear country.
- Ask God to lead us to make proper analysis of the challenges and arrive at the best possible solutions within the shortest possible time.

COLLECTIVE ACTION

Judges 5:15-18 NLT

“The princes of Issachar were with Deborah and Barak.They followed Barak, rushing into the valley. But in the tribe of Reuben there was great indecision. Why did you sit at home among the sheepfolds—to hear the shepherds whistle for their flocks? Yes, in the tribe of Reuben there was great indecision. Gilead remained east of the Jordan. And why did Dan stay home? Asher sat unmoved at the seashore, remaining in his harbors. But Zebulun risked his life, as did Naphtali, on the heights of the battlefield."

1 Samuel 14:6

"And Jonathan said to the young man that bare his armour, Come, and let us go over unto the garrison of these uncircumcised: it may be that the Lord will work for us: for there is no restraint to the LORD to save by many or by few."

Deborah and Barak led the Israelites to war against the Canaanites who were led by the commander Sisera but not everyone joined in. The Reubenites were stuck in ANALYSIS PARALYSIS (should a woman lead us, should we join our fellow countrymen, should we go our separate ways, should we attack from the left or right, should we attack today or wait for full moon?) until the war was over. Gilead remained in his geopolitical zone of the East, the Danites became stay-at-home warriors, while the tribe of Asher were stuck in their ships .

The great thing was that though not all fought in the battle yet the victory was declared for the whole country. That's why the reluctant ones were 'called out' and of course they joined in the subsequent campaigns.

Prayer Point 4

- Pray that we will be empowered by heaven to take COLLECTIVE ACTION and NOT BE HESITANT or become like the Reubenites analysing without corresponding action.
- Pray that as we ACT heaven WILL SEND HELP beyond our expectations.
- Pray that as we ACT confusion will descend into the camp of the enemy and they will be discombobulated and confused.
- Pray earnestly that we will Converge, Connect, Converse and take Collective Action as a people united in purpose.

18
BINDING THE STRONG
MAN AND EMPOWERING
NIGERIA'S GUARDIAN
ANGEL

CHAPTER EIGHTEEN
PRAYER DAY 18

BINDING THE STRONG MAN AND EMPOWERING NIGERIA'S GUARDIAN ANGEL

Prayer Quote

"The one concern of the devil is to keep Christians from praying. He fears nothing from prayerless studies, prayerless work and prayerless religion. He laughs at our toil, mocks at our wisdom, but he trembles when we pray." Samuel Chadwick.

WE DO NOT WAR AFTER THE FLESH

2 Corinthians 10:3-6

"For though we walk in the flesh, we do not war after the flesh: (For the weapons of our warfare are not carnal, but mighty through God to the pulling down of strong holds ;) Casting down imaginations, and every high thing that exalteth itself against the knowledge of God, and bringing into captivity every thought to the obedience of Christ; And having in a readiness to revenge all disobedience, when your obedience is fulfilled."

Ephesians 6:10-13

"Finally, my brethren, be strong in the Lord, and in the power of his might. Put on the whole armour of God that ye may be able to stand against the wiles of the devil.

For we wrestle not against flesh and blood, but against principalities, against powers, against the rulers of the darkness of this world, against

spiritual wickedness in high places.
Wherefore take unto you the whole armour of God that ye may be able to withstand in the evil day, and having done all, to stand."

Let's be reminded today where our strength comes from

No matter how tempted we are to act in the flesh we must remember:
Old testament saints waged war primarily in the physical realm but we in the New Testament wage war primarily in the spiritual realm
The fact is the Old Testament saints couldn't address spiritual entities as Christ had not yet redeemed man but after the cross He gave us His authority to tread on all powers of the enemy and nothing shall by any means hurt us.
Thus our assignment is much higher than that of Old Testament saints.

Prayer Point 1

- Ask God to open our eyes to the incredible power available to us to wage war in the spiritual realm.
- Ask for His grace for us to operate a life of complete obedience to His Word, His Will and His Way.
- That we will withstand every wile and trickery from hell.
- That we will stand firm in the whole armour of God.

DEMONIC PRINCES OVER NATIONS

Daniel10:12-13

"Then he said to me, "Do not fear, Daniel, for from the first day that you set your heart to understand, and to humble yourself before your God, your words were heard; and I have come because of your words. But the prince of the kingdom of Persia withstood me twenty-one days; and behold, Michael, one of the chief princes, came to help me, for I had been left alone there with the kings of Persia."

The above text clearly revealed that there was a demonic prince assigned over the natural kingdom of Persia.
This angel speaking in our text could not be referring to the physical prince of Persia for no natural man can pose such a challenge to an angel.
Notice that initially the angel was actually outnumbered: 'for I had been LEFT ALONE there with the KINGS of Persia.
It also reveals that the angel was dispatched ONLY at the instance of Daniel's actions in the place of fasting and seeking the face of the Lord for his nation for the angel said: 'I have come because of your words'."

At this time in our twenty one Day prayer effort, it's important to ask "are we over spiritualizing the issue of Nigeria or are we underestimating the organizational structure and determination of hell to hold us down?"
The book of Daniel provides a rare peak into how interwoven the spirit realm is with the natural. It shows that if Daniel did not persevere in the place of prayer he may not have received the breakthrough he did.
There was also a corresponding relationship between Daniel's prayers and the activation of additional angelic reinforcement. Archangel Michael himself. (This was some heavy-duty stuff).
This should encourage us to know that if we stay faithful upon our prayer watch we will be activating higher activities of God's angelic forces that otherwise may not have been activated.
This does NOT suggest we communicate directly with angels but rather it's a reminder that what we are doing in prayer has tremendous impact in the

realm of the spirit.....perhaps much more than we may ever know.
Can you imagine that the demonic prince of Persia actually had the EFFRONTERY to intercept and delay a messenger sent by God Himself? Well such is the manner of the enemy we face!

Prayer Point 2

- Pray that God will activate his powerful angels on assignment because of our words like in the case of Daniel.
- That we will not give up on our watch but hang in there until we obtain the necessary help from heaven to overrun the demonic prince and his demonic cohorts operating over our nation.

GOD'S ANGELS ASSIGNED OVER NATIONS

Daniel 10:20-21
"Then he said, Do you know why I have come to you? And now I will return to fight with the [hostile] prince of Persia; and when I have gone, behold, the [hostile] prince of Greece will come.
But I will tell you what is inscribed in the writing of truth or the Book of Truth. There is no one who holds with me and strengthens himself against these [hostile spirit forces] except Michael, your prince [national guardian angel]."

Another stunning truth revealed here is that the Archangel Michael is actually the national guardian angel of the physical nation of Israel.
This means that the devil's kingdom is just imitating God's divine order, for the enemy is no originator he is just an imitator.
So it follows that if Satan has assigned a prince over Nigeria that surely there is an angelic prince assigned by God over Nigeria, just as in the case

of Israel that in spite of their guardian angels they still suffer major setbacks so also Nigeria will continue to suffer more from the influence of the demonic prince than benefit from our national guardian angel EXCEPT we the Daniels of our day do something to turn the tables around.

Prayer Point 3

- Pray that God will send angelic reinforcements to strengthen the angelic prince He has assigned over Nigeria
- Ask God to help us work in harmony with His angelic forces assigned over Nigeria.
- Pray that we will provide the required sacrifices appropriate to overturning the stubborn prince over Nigeria.

FIRST BIND THE STRONGMAN

Mark 3:27

"No man can enter into a strongman's house, and spoil his goods, except he will first bind the strongman; and then he will spoil his house."

Luke 11:21-22

"When a strongman armed keepeth his palace, his goods are in peace: But when a stronger than he shall come upon him, and overcome him, he taketh from him all his armour wherein he trusted, and divideth his spoils."

Jesus in the above scriptures gave us clear strategies on how to tackle the strongman.
First bind the strongman.

Then spoil his goods. (The catch is that you must be stronger than the strong man).

Prayer Point 4

- Pray that we generate enough power in the spirit realm to bind the strongman over Nigeria and that we plunder his goods.
- Let's proceed and strip the strongman of all his armor which he trusts.
- Pray strong in the spirit, for the effectual fervent prayer of the righteous availeth much.
- Give God thanks that we have the victory like Daniel did in his 21 Day prayer effort. Ours may take longer or shorter but either way we shall not relent until we taste the victory.

19

DEALING A HARD BLOW AGAINST THE CULTURE OF CORRUPTION

CHAPTER NINETEEN
PRAYER DAY 19

DEALING A HARD BLOW AGAINST THE CULTURE OF CORRUPTION

Prayer Quote

"I would rather teach one man to pray than ten men to preach." Charles Spurgeon

PROPHESY AGAINST THE CULTURE OF THE CORRUPTION

Psalm 73:3-12

"For I was envious at the foolish, when I saw the prosperity of the wicked. For there are no bands in their death: but their strength is firm. They are not in trouble as other men; neither are they plagued like other men. Therefore pride compasseth them about as a chain; violence covereth them as a garment. Their eyes stand out with fatness: they have more than heart could wish. They are corrupt, and speak wickedly concerning oppression: they speak loftily. They set their mouth against the heavens, and their tongue walketh through the earth. Therefore his people return hither: and waters of a full cup are wrung out to them. And they say, how doth God know? And is there knowledge in the most High? Behold, these are the ungodly, who prosper in the world; they increase in riches."

Finally we can address a familiar foe. CORRUPTION. At the end of the day, as long as this monster continues to be tolerated, celebrated and worshipped, there is no hope for Nigeria.

Dictionary definition of Corrupt: Guilty of dishonest practices, as bribery; lacking integrity crooked: a corrupt judge.
Debased in character; depraved; perverted; wicked; evil: a corrupt society.

The above definitions on corruption gave two examples...a corrupt judge and a corrupt society....that's the worst combination any society can have, sadly speaking we are faced with this double jeopardy.
If the system is corrupt and the ones responsible to correct the system are the ones perpetuating 'Mr Corruption's' long term in office, then there is no hope for the nation.

Prayer Point 1

- Prayerfully dismantle and uproot the culture of corruption in Nigeria. That the corrupt who delight in wickedness, oppression, violence and arrogantly speak against the Most High will get a swift reply from God.
- That the righteous will stop being envious of the wicked but be empowered with wealth and wisdom to lead.
- That the righteous will ever be mindful to be faithful and to use their wealth to right the wrongs in our society.
- That the mindset of corruption that has eaten deeply into EVERY aspect of our society from the government to the governed, from the legislator to the solicitor, from the judge to the judged, from the boardroom to the classroom, from the minister to the trader, that such mindset will receive a SHOCK treatment from the INCORRUPTIBLE Judge who seats enthroned in the heavens!

PROPHESY AGAINST THE CORRUPT

Ezekiel 11:1-2,

"Moreover the spirit lifted me up, and brought me unto the east gate of the Lord's house, which looketh eastward: and behold at the door of the gate five and twenty men; among whom I saw Jaazaniah the son of Azur, and PELATIAH THE SON OF BENAIAH, princes of the people. Then said he unto me, Son of man, these are the men that devise mischief, and give wicked counsel in this city:"

Ezekiel 11:4

"Therefore prophesy against them, prophesy, O son of man."

Ezekiel 11:13a

"And it came to pass, when I prophesied, that PELATIAH THE SON OF BENAIAH died."

Prophet Ezekiel had a revelation and saw the 25 highly placed princes behind the misfortune of the nation.

The prophet was COMMANDED to prophesy against them and his prophecy proceeded with such pin point accuracy that one of them died instantly as he prophesied.

Prayer Point 2

- Declare that God's judgment will proceed with pin point accuracy and judge the principal personalities perpetuating the culture of corruption in Nigeria.
- The Wicked Wasters shall not stand in the day of God's judgment.

Psalms 37:20

"But the wicked shall perish, and the enemies of the Lord shall be as the fat of lambs: they shall consume; into smoke shall they consume away."

Psalms 68:2

"As smoke is driven away, so drive them away: as wax melteth before the fire, so let the wicked perish at the presence of God."

Proverbs 10:28

"The hope of the righteous shall be gladness: but the expectation of the wicked shall perish."

Proverbs 11:10

"When it goes well with the [uncompromisingly] righteous, the city rejoices, but when the wicked perish, there are shouts of joy."

Proverbs 28:28

"When the wicked rise, men hide themselves: but when they perish, the righteous increase."

Psalms 73:16-20 (Amplified)

"But when I considered how to understand this, it was too great an effort for me and too painful until I went into the sanctuary of God; then I understood [for I considered] their end. [After all] You do set the [wicked] in slippery places; you cast them down to ruin and destruction. How they become a desolation in a moment! They are utterly consumed with terrors! As a dream [which seems real] until one awakens, so, O Lord, when you arouse yourself [to take note of the wicked], you will despise their outward show."

Prayer Point 3

- Pray with the above passages as you are led.
- LET THE RIGHTEOUS REIGN IN NIGERIA

Ezekiel 21:27

"I will overturn, overturn, overturn, it: and it shall be no more, until he come whose right it is; and I will give it him."

Prov 29:2

"When the [uncompromisingly] righteous are in authority, the people rejoice; but when the wicked man rules, the people groan and sigh."

Prov 29:4 (MSG)

"A leader of good judgment gives stability; an exploiting leader leaves a trail of waste."

Prov 29:4 (NIV)

"By justice a king gives a country stability, but those who are greedy for bribes tear it down."

1 Timothy 6:10

"For the love of money is the root of all evil: which while some coveted after, they have erred from the faith, and pierced themselves through with many sorrows."

Prayer Point 4

- Cry out to the LORD and ask that the corrupt and wicked will no longer hold the reins of influence or authority in Nigeria but that they will fade away like an old garment.(we recognize this may take a few years but let the process begin now).

- That they will not be replaced by another generation of wicked WASTERS.
- That God will turn the tables around and around until the uncompromisingly righteous are in full authority.
- That God will raise Josephs, Daniels, Davids, Esthers and Deborahs to take charge of the affairs of our nation....and most importantly that we will NOT lack these God fearing men and women in leadership positions in our land.
- Pray that these godly REFORMERS will be empowered and emboldened to take charge in this season.

20

NEW SHARP INSTRUMENTS IN HIS HANDS

CHAPTER TWENTY
PRAYER DAY 20

NEW SHARP INSTRUMENTS IN HIS HANDS

Prayer Quote

On persevering prayer:

"I look at a stone cutter hammering away at a rock a hundred times without so much as a crack showing in it. Yet at the 101st blow it splits in two. I know it was not the one blow that did it, but all that had gone before."

Key Scripture

Isaiah 41:15

"Behold, I will make thee a new sharp threshing instrument having teeth: thou shalt thresh the mountains, and beat them small, and shalt make the hills as chaff"

An Intense Prayer Season Ushers in A New Season

1 Kings 18:41-42

"And Elijah said unto Ahab, Get thee up, eat and drink; for there is a sound of abundance of rain. So Ahab went up to eat and to drink. And Elijah went up to the top of Carmel; and he cast himself down upon the earth, and put his face between his knees,"

When the season changed, Elijah announced it to King Ahab and then he went up to the top of the mountain to PUSH (Prayed Until Something Happened). He prayed till what he sensed in his spirit could be made manifest in the physical realm.

Prayer Point 1

- Pray that The Lord will enable us as Watchmen to birth in the tangible realm the new season that we sense so strong in our spirits concerning Nigeria.
- Ask God for an overwhelming outpouring of His Spirit upon Nigeria so that He completes the birthing process of a New Nation.
- Pray that we will stay strong upon the mountain of prayer until we see all that we are now all sensing so well.

To Everything, There is a Season

Ecclesiastes 3:1

"To everything there is a season, and a time to every purpose under the heaven:"

It's time to release everything that has come into its season

Prayer Point 2

- Declare that we will not miss this opportunity, proclaim that we as a generation will not miss this window heaven has opened to step into a fresh dimension of God's divine purpose.
- Pray that we will experience absolutely everything God has for us at this time and nothing of what God has designed for us will be missing

God's chosen

Isaiah 41:8-9

"But thou, Israel, art my servant, Jacob whom I have chosen, the seed of Abraham my friend. Thou whom I have taken from the ends of the earth, and called thee from the chief men thereof, and said unto thee, Thou art my servant; I have chosen thee, and not cast thee away."

Isaiah 41:10-14

"Fear thou not; for I am with thee: be not dismayed; for I am thy God: I will strengthen thee; yea, I will help thee; yea, I will uphold thee with the right hand of my righteousness. Behold, all they that were incensed against thee shall be ashamed and confounded: they shall be as nothing; and they that strive with thee shall perish. Thou shalt seek them, and shalt not find them, even them that contended with thee: they that war against thee shall be as nothing, and as a thing of nought. For I the LORD thy God will hold thy right hand, saying unto thee, Fear not; I will help thee. Fear not, thou worm Jacob, and ye men of Israel; I will help thee, saith the LORD, and thy redeemer, the Holy One of Israel."

The Lord has gone through great lengths to preserve us till this day as a nation.

Many had written us off and given 'prophecies' that we will be a failed state.

All these lies telling us about hell's agenda for Nigeria have not succeeded because our promise and prophecy in God as a nation and as a people is far greater.

Prayer Point 3

- Declare that God has chosen you and has not cast you away.
- Praise the Lord because He has assured you of His presence all the time.
- Rebuke the spirit of fear and insist it will not have a foothold in your life whatsoever.
- Declare that all those that have risen against you shall fall for your sake and they shall fall and disappear without a trace.
- Pray that even in times when you feel like a worm and feel too insignificant you will remember you matter to God deeply.

God's New Sharp Threshing Instrument

Isaiah 41:15-20

"Behold, I will make thee a new sharp threshing instrument having teeth: thou shalt thresh the mountains, and beat them small, and shalt make the hills as chaff. Thou shalt fan them, and the wind shall carry them away, and the whirlwind shall scatter them: and thou shalt rejoice in the LORD, and shalt glory in the Holy One of Israel. When the poor and needy seek water, and there is none, and their tongue faileth for thirst, I the LORD will hear them, I the God of Israel will not forsake them. I will open rivers in high places, and fountains in the midst of the valleys: I will make the wilderness a pool of water, and the dry land springs of water. I will plant in the wilderness the cedar, the shittah tree, and the myrtle, and the oil tree; I will set in the desert the fir tree, and the pine, and the box tree together: That they may see, and know, and consider, and understand together, that the hand of the LORD hath done this, and the Holy One of Israel hath created it."

As we have embarked on this prayer initiative the Lord is using it to sharpen us and make us into new Sharp threshing instruments.

Prayer Point 4

- Prayerfully beat down every mountain and all insurmountable obstacles that previously had defied all solutions.
- Pray for new insight, new strength and an incredible power from the Lord to do damage to the kingdom of darkness.
- Thank God that He is turning our wilderness into a garden of abundance
- Declare that the Hand of the Lord is behind our newness and not our ability or our intelligence.

Understanding and Redeeming the Times

1 Chronicles 12:32

"And of the children of Issachar, which were men that had understanding of the times, to know what Israel ought to do; the heads of them were two hundred; and all their brethren were at their commandment."

Psalms 102:13

"Thou shalt arise, and have mercy upon Zion: for the time to favour her, yea, the set time, is come."

Leviticus 26:3-4

"If ye walk in my statutes, and keep my commandments, and do them; Then I will give you rain in due season, and the land shall yield her increase, and the trees of the field shall yield their fruit."

People of understanding are the ones who become outstanding.
We must redeem the time and maximize our set time 'kairos' moment.

Prayer Point 5

- Pray that just like the children of Issachar had understanding of the times whilst others did not, that we as a people will discern God's corporate purpose for us at this time and cooperate fully with heaven.
- Ask the Lord to give you an accurate understanding of the specific purpose and role you ought to play in the place He has assigned for you in your city, sector, community and in the nation.
- Ask The Lord to help you not just to sense His purposes that have come into fruition but to KNOW what to do.
- Pray that a whole new level of divine authority will be released upon us as a people just like the children of Issachar because of the spirit of understanding that is upon us.
- Pray that we will spend our time wisely even in this 'kairos' moment (set time) that God has brought us into.
- Come against every time waster and anything that wants to distract you at this time from maximizing the moment.
- Ask for God's grace to be disciplined in your time management in this season.

DECLARATIONS AND BLESSINGS

CHAPTER TWENTY ONE
PRAYER DAY 21

DECLARATIONS AND BLESSINGS

Prayer Quote

"Prayer is the greatest of all forces, because it honors God and brings him into active aid." E.M. Bounds

Let's pronounce blessings upon our nation and upon every watchman as well as give thanks to God for a successful prayer campaign!

Personalize and declare the following blessings upon our nation and ourselves.

Deuteronomy 33:6-30

"Let Reuben live, and not die; and let not his men be few. And this is the blessing of Judah: and he said, Hear, Lord, the voice of Judah, and bring him unto his people: let his hands be sufficient for him; and be thou an help to him from his enemies. And of Levi he said. (edited) They shall teach Jacob thy judgments, and Israel thy law: they shall put incense before thee, and whole burnt sacrifice upon thine altar. Bless, Lord, his substance, and accept the work of his hands: smite through the loins of them that rise against him, and of them that hate him that they rise not again. And of Benjamin he said, the beloved of the Lord shall dwell in safety by him; and the LORD shall cover him all the day long, and he shall dwell between his shoulders. And of Joseph he said, Blessed of the Lord be his land, for the precious things of heaven, for the dew, and for the deep that coucheth beneath, And for the precious fruits brought forth by the sun, and for the precious things put forth by the moon, And for the chief things of the ancient mountains, and for the precious things of the lasting hills, And for the precious things of the earth and fullness thereof, and for the good will of him that dwelt in the bush: let the blessing come upon the head of Joseph, and upon the top of the head of him that was separated from his brethren. And of Zebulun he said, Rejoice, Zebulun, in thy going out; and, Issachar, in thy tents. They shall call the people unto the mountain; there they shall offer sacrifices of righteousness: for they shall suck of the abundance of the seas, and of treasures hid in the sand. And of Gad he said, Blessed be he that enlargeth Gad: he dwelleth as a lion, and teareth the arm with the crown of the head. And he provided the first part for himself, because there, in a portion of the lawgiver, was he seated; and he came with the heads of the people, he executed the justice of the Lord, and his judgments with Israel. And of Dan he said, Dan is a lion's whelp: he shall leap from Bashan. And of Naphtali he said, O Naphtali, satisfied with favour, and full with the blessing of the Lord: possess thou the west and the south. And of Asher he said, Let Asher be blessed with children; let him be acceptable to his brethren, and let him dip his foot in oil. Thy shoes shall be iron and brass; and as thy days, so shall thy strength be."

AND OF NIGERIA.....SAY

*There is none like unto the God of Jeshurun, *(Nigeria) who rideth upon the heaven in thy help, and in his Excellency on the sky. The eternal God is thy refuge, and underneath are the everlasting arms: and he shall thrust out the enemy from before thee; and shall say, Destroy them. Israel *(Nigeria) then shall dwell in safety alone: the fountain of Jacob *(Nigeria) shall be upon a land of corn and wine; also his heavens shall drop down dew.*

* Nigeria in above text added by author for emphasis only

*Happy art thou, O Israel *(Nigeria): who is like unto thee, O people saved by the Lord, the shield of thy help, and who is the sword of thy Excellency! And thine enemies shall be found liars unto thee; and thou shalt tread upon their high places.*

Now Give Thanks to God

Thank Him for His strength throughout these 21 days.

Thank Him for Victory is assured.

Thank Him that the watchmen, warriors and wise ones in Nigeria have risen to their responsibilities.

Thank Him that the worried ones have been delivered.

Thank Him that the wasters have been brought to justice and made irrelevant in Nigeria.

Thank Him that the reins of power have shifted from the wasters to the wise ones and warriors.

Thank Him that you are part of the reformation effort of this generation and that you will be found faithful as a SPEARMAN like Joshua.

Thank Him for all the CONVERGENCE, CONNECTIONS, CONVERSATIONS, and COLLECTIVE ACTIONS we will need to carry out will not be in vain.

Thank Him for me and you and for grace He has given us to fulfil our roles within the context of His call upon us!

Go ahead and thank Him as you are; shout, sing, dance etc...

Give thanks as you feel led by His Spirit at this time.

Psalms 149

"Praise ye the Lord. Sing unto the LORD a new song, and his praise in the congregation of saints.

Let Israel rejoice in him that made him: let the children of Zion be joyful in

their King.
Let them praise his name in the dance: let them sing praises unto him with the timbrel and harp.
For the Lord taketh pleasure in his people: he will beautify the meek with salvation.
Let the saints be joyful in glory: let them sing aloud upon their beds.
Let the high praises of God be in their mouth, and a two-edged sword in their hand;
To execute vengeance upon the heathen, and punishments upon the people;
To bind their kings with chains, and their nobles with fetters of iron;
To execute upon them the judgment written: this honour have all his saints.
Praise ye the Lord."

Psalms 150

"Praise ye the Lord. Praise God in his sanctuary: praise him in the firmament of his power.
Praise him for his mighty acts: praise him according to his excellent greatness.
Praise him with the sound of the trumpet: praise him with the psaltery and harp
Praise him with the timbrel and dance: praise him with stringed instruments and organs.
Praise him upon the loud cymbals: praise him upon the high sounding cymbals.
Let everything that hath breath praise the Lord. Praise ye the LORD."

CONCLUSION

PRAY AND ACT

Nigeria has a definite divine promise over her. It's up to us as citizens to activate and insist on our knees first and then fold our sleeves to Converge, Connect, Converse and take Collective action.

Daniel shows us this is possible and in his case they were only a few good men with him. The minority report is enough as long as they know how to connect to heaven.

It does not take much to actually trigger an avalanche on a mountaintop. All it takes is for a few 'little snow flakes' to act on the previous build-up of other little snowflakes.

However, once the avalanche begins, it is UNSTOPPABLE!

God bless you!!

God bless our beloved country NIGERIA!!!

CONCLUSION

PRAY AND ACT

EPILOGUE

HOW GOD VISITS HIS PEOPLE

There are always three (3) critical elements present when God wants to bring about His divine visitation among any people.

Malachi 3:1-6.

"Behold, I am going to send My messenger, and he will prepare and clear the way before Me. And the Lord [the Messiah], whom you seek, will suddenly come to His temple; the Messenger of the covenant, in whom you delight, behold, He is coming," says the Lord of hosts. But who can endure the day of His coming? And who can stand when He appears? For He is like a refiner's fire and like launderer's soap [which removes impurities and uncleanness]. He will sit as a refiner and purifier of silver, and He will purify the sons of Levi [the priests], and refine them like gold and silver, so that they may present to the Lord [grain] offerings in righteousness. Then the offering of Judah and Jerusalem will be pleasing to the Lord as in the days of old and as in ancient years.

"Then I will come near you for judgment; I will be a swift witness against sorcerers, against adulterers, against perjurers, and against those who oppress the laborer in his wages and widows and the fatherless, and against those who turn away the alien [from his right], and those who do not fear Me [with awe-filled reverence]," says the Lord of hosts. "For I am the Lord, I do not change [but remain faithful to My covenant with you]; that is why you, O sons of Jacob, have not come to an end."

The threefold order of divine visitation is Prophetic Stirrings, Priestly

Intercessions and Kingly Decrees.

Prophetic Stirring

In the Malachi text above, first God says He will send His messenger (prophet) who will clear and prepare the way for the MESSENGER (Messiah).

"Behold, I am going to send My messenger, and he will prepare and clear the way before Me. And the Lord [the Messiah], whom you seek, will suddenly come to His temple; the Messenger of the covenant, in whom you delight, behold, He is coming," says the Lord of hosts."

In the first fulfillment of this particular prophecy the messenger referred to in small caps was John the Baptist, who went ahead of the MESSENGER - The Lord Jesus. This is always the first step in God's divine visitation. The prophetic prepares the way of the Lord and also prepares the heart of the people for God's visitation so that the people will be ready when He comes. That's why He asked in verse 2 who can stand when He appears?

But who can endure the day of His coming? And who can stand when He appears? For He is like a refiner's fire and like launderer's soap [which removes impurities and uncleanness].

Priestly Intercession

This prophetic stirring is what breaks the dead spiritual silence and ushers in the next step, which is the season of Priestly Intercession. This is seen in verse 3...

He will sit as a refiner and purifier of silver, and He will purify the sons of Levi [the priests], and refine them like gold and silver, so that they may present to the Lord [grain] offerings in righteousness.

The sons of Levi refers to our role as intercessors, which in the New Testament is for all saints. When the prophetic hits the people of God they go into an intense season of protracted and sustained intercessions. That is of course, if God can find a willing and able people to work with. This is a refining phase and critical to ensuring the people are purified and made ready like silver and are prepared for final use.

Kingly Decree

The last step is when the church effectively enters into her kingly role of being able to make decrees and declarations over the land and they actually stick.

Then the offering of Judah and Jerusalem will be pleasing to the Lord as in the days of old and as in ancient years.

Judah and Jerusalem refers to the kingly role of the church, as Judah is the kingly tribe that ushered in the King of kings, while Jerusalem is His eternal Capital City whether on earth or as New Jerusalem during His Millennial reign.
If the people of God bypass any of this divine order, then they will be ineffective in bringing about the necessary change as required by heaven.

Every Divine Visitation is a Time of Divine Judgment

God's Word is a two-edged sword so as God brings about a visitation, it invariably comes with His judgment on those who have oppressed or stood in His way to blessing His people.

It was the same in the time of Moses, the emancipation of God's people from their bondage in Egypt could only happen with a total defeat and near annihilation of their oppressors. That's just how the cookie always crumbles.

"Then I will come near you for judgment; I will be a swift witness against sorcerers, against adulterers, against perjurers, and against those who oppress the laborer in his wages and widows and the fatherless, and against those who turn away the alien [from his right], and those who do not fear Me [with awe-filled reverence]," says the Lord of hosts. 6 "For I am the Lord, I do not change [but remain faithful to My covenant with you]; that is why you, O sons of Jacob, have not come to an end."

The Queen Esther and Prime Minister Mordecai Example

Esther 4:5-9

"Then Esther sent for Hathach, one of the king's eunuchs who had been appointed as her attendant. She ordered him to go to Mordecai and find out what was troubling him and why he was in mourning. So Hathach went out to Mordecai in the square in front of the palace gate.

Mordecai told him the whole story, including the exact amount of money Haman had promised to pay into the royal treasury for the destruction of the

Jews. Mordecai gave Hathach a copy of the decree issued in Susa that called for the death of all Jews. He asked Hathach to show it to Esther and explain the situation to her. He also asked Hathach to direct her to go to the king to beg for mercy and plead for her people. So Hathach returned to Esther with Mordecai's message.

Then Esther told Hathach to go back and relay this message to Mordecai: “All the king's officials and even the people in the provinces know that anyone who appears before the king in his inner court without being invited is doomed to die unless the king holds out his gold scepter. And the king has not called for me to come to him for thirty days.”

Queen Esther's Prophetic Stirring

Mordecai is in mourning and his niece queen Esther sends a messenger to find out why. He tells the messenger that a decree has been issued that will exterminate her people on March the 7th the following year. Her reply is typical of a cold, disconnected believer whose personal well-being has disconnected them from the plight of the majority. Esther sends back a nonchalant reply to her uncle and tells him how potentially risky it was for her to break palace protocol to enter the king’s presence uninvited, in fact it could cost her life. So it's not a risk she could possibly take.

However, Mordecai sends back a sharp rebuke that seems to suddenly jolt and stir her up prophetically. He rebukes her for not seeing the urgency of the moment and ends by saying these famous words.."who knows if you are in the kingdom for such a time as this?"

Esther 4:13-14

Mordecai sent this reply to Esther: “Don't think for a moment that because you're in the palace you will escape when all other Jews are killed. If you keep quiet at a time like this, deliverance and relief for the Jews will arise from some other place, but you and your relatives will die. Who knows if perhaps you were made queen for just such a time as this?"

Suddenly the cold sounding queen Esther shifts as the prophetic words from Mordecai stirs her deeply and reminds her of why God had placed her in the palace in the first place. That's exactly what the prophetic stirring is all about and why it's the first step towards a divine visitation or in this case a divine intervention.

The Jews engage in Priestly Intercession

This 180 degrees turn takes Esther into the next step as she calls for a 3-day fast for all the Jews in Susa.

Esther 4:15-16

Then Esther sent this reply to Mordecai: 16 "Go and gather together all the Jews of Susa and fast for me. Do not eat or drink for three days, night or day. My maids and I will do the same. And then, though it is against the law, I will go in to see the king. If I must die, I must die."

Notice that Mordecai was not the one that called for a fast but Esther. How could someone who was so disconnected at the beginning of the chapter suddenly go from zero to hero? Well that's exactly what the prophetic is able to accomplish. One well placed prophetic wake up call was all it took to jerk our heroin Queen Esther to making perhaps one of the most famous statements in the Bible.

Esther 4:16 KJV

"...and if I perish, I perish."

It was in this period that Esther was able to come up with a strategy on how best to approach the king on the matter. If she had rushed in the first time she got the message without this intercessory pause, I believe the results would not have been as strong or may even have fallen on deaf ears. We as believers must never underestimate the power of heartfelt fervent prayers born out of a strong prophetic unction.

Mordecai making Kingly Decree

The result of the short but intense prayer season is met with initial success as Haman the hunter, suddenly became the hunted as both heaven and earth conspired against him. So Haman is hanged on the very tall gallows he had made for Mordecai the day before.

Esther 7:9-10

"Then Harbona, one of the king's eunuchs, said, "Haman has set up a sharpened pole that stands seventy-five feet tall in his own courtyard. He intended to use it to impale Mordecai, the man who saved the king from assassination." "Then impale Haman on it!" the king ordered. So they impaled Haman on the pole he had set up for Mordecai, and the king's anger subsided."

However, his evil plot to commit the first genocide in the history of mankind is not yet over as Haman had locked it up in a decree that had been sealed in the king's signet ring which made it irreversible.

The only way this could be resolved was made possible not through prophetic stirring or priestly intercession but by the 3rd step: Kingly Decree.

Esther 8:9-12

"So on June 25 the king's secretaries were summoned, and a decree was written exactly as Mordecai dictated. It was sent to the Jews and to the highest officers, the governors, and the nobles of all the 127 provinces stretching from India to Ethiopia. The decree was written in the scripts and languages of all the peoples of the empire, including that of the Jews. The decree was written in the name of King Xerxes and sealed with the king's signet ring. Mordecai sent the dispatches by swift messengers, who rode fast horses especially bred for the king's service. The king's decree gave the Jews in every city authority to unite to defend their lives. They were allowed to kill, slaughter, and annihilate anyone of any nationality or province who might attack them or their children and wives, and to take the property of their enemies. The day chosen for this event throughout all the provinces of King Xerxes was March 7 of the next year."

The only solution to neutralize the evil decree of Haman was to make a superceeding decree to be executed on the very same day Haman had carefully selected through sorcery. This was spiritual warfare at a whole new level.

Mordecai the Prime Minister

Esther 10:3

"Mordecai the Jew became the prime minister, with authority next to that of King Xerxes himself. He was very great among the Jews, who held him in high esteem, because he continued to work for the good of his people and to speak up for the welfare of all their descendants."

The book of Esther starts with Mordecai as a palace attendant with no title and ends 10 chapters later with him being the second most powerful man in the entire empire of 127 provinces. It's amazing how his role shifted throughout this account. At the beginning of the book he would not have been considered the main character as even the book is not named after him but after his niece Esther. However as the story unfolds, the reader soon realizes that everything actually revolved around Mordecai. From the upbringing of his niece after she was orphaned at a young age, to her ending up in the palace as queen. Mordecai was the major instrument God used. The saga that was the climax of the story all began with an attitude Mordecai had towards a proud and powerful highly placed official in the king's court...Haman. His role in saving the king from an asssination attempt and his being saved a few hours before facing the gallows are all evidence that Mordecai was specially blessed by the God of Abraham.

Mordecai gave the very statement that released the prophetic stirring in sharp rebuke of his somewhat reluctant niece. At the end Mordecai did not only partake in the threefold order of divine visitation of Prophetic Stirring, Priestly Intercession and Kingly Decree but he was the main point person for their manifestations.

This is exactly what happens when God visits His people, it's like a two-edged sword. On the one side those who were stealing the show and oppressing the poor get the judgment side of the sword, while the righteous who have been at the receiving end get the other side of the sword that brings relief and incredible blessings.

The story ends quite befittingly with Mordecai mentioned in the closing remarks...

Esther 10:3

"Mordecai the Jew became the prime minister, with authority next to that of King Xerxes himself. He was very great among the Jews, who held him in high esteem, because he continued to work for the good of his people and to speak up for the welfare of all their descendants."

He became prime minister, second in command, very great among the Jews, held in high esteem and he continued to work for the good of his people and speak up for their welfare.

What a way to end-on such a powerful note!

Who Knows If "YOU" are in the kingdom for such as time as this?

A reader will not realize the true impact of a book like this, if they keep asking themselves what others are going to do with the message. The potency of this prophetic book is what you decide to do with it, not your neighbour, not your friend or someone you know but your role in this prophetic imperative!

Before you close this book I suggest you ask yourself the same question that stirred queen Esther's heart and made her to take a decision that altered the history of her people forever. Till this day the feast of Purim is still observed by the Jews. This was made possible because of a few ordinary people, who were at the brink of a genocide, decided to call on their extraordinary God. This story is further made interesting, as the book of Esther is the only book where the name of God is not once mentioned, although His invisible hand is seen from the start to the finish of this epic real life drama!

Esther 4:14b

"Who knows if perhaps you were made queen for just such a time as this?"

Why did God lead you to read this book at such a time as this?
Why are you a Nigerian or a friend of Nigeria at such a time as this?
Perhaps you are about to respond to the prophecies contained in this book?
Perhaps history is about to be made through your obedience to the message penned down in the pages of this book?
Who knows if you may just be the Queen Esther that Nigeria has been waiting for?
Who knows if you may just be the Prime Minister Mordecai that Nigeria has been waiting for?
Yes who knows if you are in the kingdom for such a time as this?
Who knows?

NOTES

1. Edet DI,Akinyemi AF, Edet AI, et al. *Conservation of the west African black-crowned crane balearica pavonina pavonina (linn 1758) in the sudano- sahelian wetlands of northern Nigeria.* Int J Avian & Wildlife Biol. 2018;3(1):15–19. DOI: 10.15406/ijawb.2018.03.00045

2. Dake FJ. *Dake's Annotated Reference Bible*. 715 p.

3. Dake FJ. *Dake's Annotated Reference Bible*. 515 p.

4. Eugene T. *Shared Values*. National Library Board of Singapore website accessed 17 September 2018:
https://eresources.nlb.gov.sg/infopedia/articles/SIP_542_2004-12-18.html

OTHER BOOKS BY AUTHOR

Missing in Action- The Fatherhood Crisis

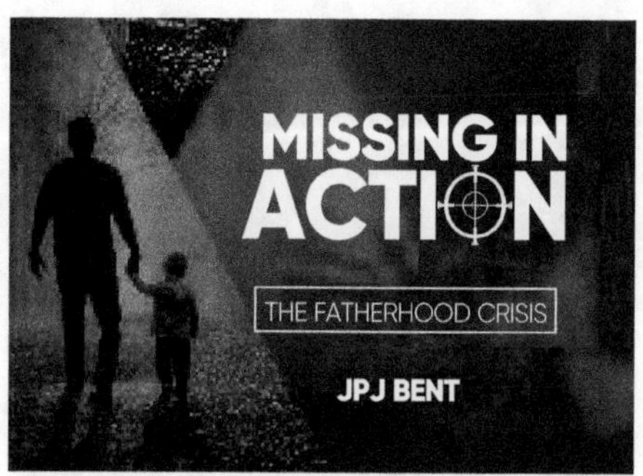

Description

This amazing photo book unlike the conventional norm is presented in contemporary style designed to convey its powerful message, with images and well crafted words to keep you flipping through till the end. It's central message: FATHERHOOD IN CRISIS...but there is a way out!

The world is in desperate need of true fathers more than any other group of professionals, more than therapists, politicians, educators or motivational speakers.

In the past fatherhood was a thing of pride but sadly in recent decades the tabloids are full of headlines about the "sins of the fathers", sexual scandals and other dishonourable acts by men in high places who were regarded as heroes but ended up as zeroes in modelling true fatherhood. Children, mothers, wives, and society at large are crying out for responsible fathers. Will the men be MISSING IN ACTION (MIA) or rise up to the occasion and be MIGHTY IN ACTION?

AUTHOR'S CONTACT DETAILS

Website: www.faithpointministry.org
Email: info@faithpointministry.org

www.ingramcontent.com/pod-product-compliance
Lightning Source LLC
LaVergne TN
LVHW052023080426
835513LV00018B/2129

* 9 7 8 0 6 2 0 8 1 9 3 3 6 *